_____ lieff St.
Dunfermline,
Fife

TRUST ACCOUNTANCY

BY

CHARLES A. SCOTT, C.A.

WITH A FOREWORD

BY

WILLIAM ANNAN, M.A., C.A.

PROFESSOR OF ACCOUNTING AND BUSINESS
METHOD, UNIVERSITY OF EDINBURGH

OLIVER AND BOYD
EDINBURGH: TWEEDDALE COURT
LONDON: 33 PATERNOSTER ROW, E.C.
1936

PRINTED IN GREAT BRITAIN BY
OLIVER AND BOYD LTD., EDINBURGH

CONTENTS

FOREWORD

BY

PROFESSOR WILLIAM ANNAN, M.A., C.A.

IN dealing with our own affairs it is a matter of choice whether we shall
have accounts made up at regular intervals, and if so, what form they
will take. It is different, however, when we are dealing with monies
placed in trust for other people. The question of accounting then
assumes a more serious aspect. Although there is no statutory obligation
on trustees to keep accounts of their intromissions, there is an implied
obligation to do so under Section 17 of the Trusts Act, 1921, which
provides that, on application by trustees, the Court may order the
Accountant of Court to superintend the investment and distribution of
the trust funds and to audit the accounts. There is also case law to
the effect that trustees are bound to keep clear and accurate accounts
of their intromissions and produce them for inspection by beneficiaries.

To keep clear and accurate trust accounts a knowledge of trust law
and administration is imperative. This can be acquired by practice,
but the student needs guidance, and for both law and accounting
students the author has produced a comprehensive survey of the
administration of a trust from its inception to its close, couched in
simple and popular language. Further, as a work of reference the
volume should appeal to solicitors and accountants practising in Scotland,
and probably also to many laymen who might be glad of a guide to their
duties and responsibilities when acting as executors or trustees.

If all the transactions in a trust consisted of cash receipts and payments
for behoof of one class of persons or for an individual, the framing of an
account would be a simple matter. It would be merely an account of
receipts and payments suitably classified. In practice, however, more
than one class or person is usually interested in a trust, and the receipts
and payments must be allocated accordingly. The common case is
that of fee and liferent, where, although many of the cash transactions
can be definitely assigned to either the fiar or the liferenter, there are
others which affect both and thus fall to be apportioned between them.

The author has dealt fully with this question of apportionment in
Chapters VII. and VIII. It will be seen from perusal of Chapter VII.
that there are divergent views on the question of apportionment of
dividends. Circumstances occur where it is difficult to reconcile the
rules of apportionment laid down in the Apportionment Act with
Common Law, *e.g.* the Common Law rule of *in bonis* as applied to
payments in advance, and inconsistency often arises in practice
through the interpretation of the Apportionment Act, *e.g.* in the case
of recurring payments made in portions during a year. There is
a question whether the unit of time should be the year, the half-
year or the quarter. My view is that the unit should be the period

specified in the original contract under which the payment is made. This is usually, though not invariably, a period of a year, whether it be for the leasing of property, the lending of money, or the investing in shares with fixed rates of dividends. The contract is for a specified return of so much *per annum*, and although payment of portions of rent or interest may be stipulated for at two or more dates in the year, that does not alter the original bargain and make these payments apply to shorter periods.

Unhappily the phraseology of the contracts is not always free from ambiguity. For example, it is not uncommon to find in a lease a clause to the effect that the rent will be, say, £100 per annum " to be paid at two terms in the year, Whitsunday and Martinmas, by equal portions, beginning the first term's payment thereof, £50, at the term of Martinmas next for the half-year preceding and the like sum at Whitsunday thereafter, and so on yearly and termly." These were the terms in the case of Graham (Tennent's Executor) *v.* Lawson, 35 S.L.R. 72, which is quoted, unjustifiably I think, as authority for a general adoption of the half-year instead of the year as the unit for apportioning rents.

Again, in the Royal Bank case, 12 S.L.R. 121, which is sometimes quoted as authority for adopting the half-year as a unit for apportionment of dividends, the circumstances were of a special nature, as perusal of the whole report of the case will show. An additional circumstance of importance, not mentioned in that report, is that the Bank then made up its accounts half-yearly at 14th April and 14th October. A general application of this decision is also unjustified.

Court decisions are few in number, mainly because the amount involved is small, but, such as they are, they should not be applied to particular cases unless it is evident from a perusal of the report that the circumstances are identical, or at least very similar. Under present conditions the call for the Court's intervention is not likely to increase. The nature of the possessions of the average citizen has changed. Landed proprietors instead of collecting rents, feuduties and royalties direct, now draw dividends from private companies to which they have transferred their estates, and investment income generally is now spread over the year instead of being mainly receivable at Whitsunday and Martinmas. Such changes have limited the risk of hardship to fiar or liferenter which the Apportionment Act was designed to prevent, and for that reason there is a growing tendency for testators to provide in their wills that no apportionment is to be made of income received after death.

The chapter on Income Tax (Chapter VI.) is of exceptional interest to those who are responsible for the administration of trusts at the present time, and accountants will welcome that chapter, and also Chapters XII., XIII. and XIV., on Estate Duty, Legacy Duty and Succession Duty, for reference in the course of the audit of trust accounts. Not the least useful part of the book is the series of illustrations explaining the text and the examples of complete trust accounts. These are carefully chosen, lucidly explained, and well set out.

I commend the author's work as a valuable addition to the literature on the subject.

ACKNOWLEDGMENT

THANKS are due to all those who have assisted the author in the preparation of this book, particularly Professor Annan and Mr G. T. Chiene, W.S.

ABBREVIATIONS

[*Note.*—The number prefixed in the text is the volume number.]

A.C. . . . = Law Reports—Appeal Cases.
A.T.C. . . = Accountant Tax Cases, now Annotated Tax Cases.
Beav. . . . = Beavan's Reports of Cases in Chancery.
Bing. N.C. . . = Bingham's New Cases in the Court of Common Pleas.
Ch. (or Ch.D.) . = Law Reports, Chancery Division.
D. . . . = Court of Session Cases, 2nd Series, edited by Dunlop.
F. . . . = Court of Session Cases, 5th Series, edited by Fraser.
F.A. . . . = Finance Act.
I.T. Act . . = Income Tax Act.
K.B. . . . = Law Reports, King's Bench Division.
L.T. . . . = Law Times Reports.
M. . . . = Court of Session Cases, 3rd Series, edited by Macpherson.
Paton S.C. App. = Paton's Reports of Cases decided in the House of Lords on Appeal from Scotland.
R. . . . = Court of Session Cases, 4th Series, edited by Rettie.
S. (N.E.) . . = Court of Session Cases, 1st Series, edited by Shaw (New Edition).
S.C. . . . = Session Cases.
Sim. . . . = Simon's Reports of Cases decided in the High Court of Chancery.
S.L.R. . . = Scottish Law Reporter.
S.L.T. . . = Scots Law Times.
T.C. . . . = Tax Cases.
T.L.R. . . = Times Law Reports.
Ves. . . . = Vesey's Chancery Cases.
Wight. . . = Wightwick's Reports in the Exchequer.
Y. and J. . . = Younge and Jervis's Reports of Cases in the Court of Exchequer.

TRUST ACCOUNTANCY

CHAPTER I

ADMINISTRATION OF TRUSTS

I. INTRODUCTION

ALTHOUGH the title of this book is *Trust Accountancy* it seems advisable to give here some general notes on trust administration in Scotland in order that the chapters on accountancy questions may be more readily understood. Throughout the book technicalities have been avoided so far as possible in order that the student may follow the explanations, but for certain chapters—particularly as regards death duties—a more advanced knowledge is probably required than for other chapters. Notes have been inserted as to judgments in numerous cases decided in the courts, including English decisions where these are applicable to Scotland, and statutes are also quoted for reference purposes.

II. EXECUTRY PROCEDURE

Executors are persons appointed to administer the affairs of a deceased person. Their duties consist of burial of the deceased in a suitable manner, then realising the estate and paying debts, funeral expenses, death duties and legacies. They must then pay over the residue of the estate to those entitled to share in it, or to the trustees if there is a continuing trust. In practice the executors and trustees are usually the same persons but this is not essential. {Duties of Executors.}

Executors should be named in all wills and if so appointed are known as executors-nominate. If there is none named, or if those named have previously died, or do not accept office, those named as trustees may act as executors, and failing them a residuary legatee is entitled to act. If none of these is available an executor-dative may be appointed by the court on a petition being presented to that effect. {Appointment of Executors.}

The executors should appoint a solicitor and factor to administer the estate and it is usual for one person or firm to combine these two offices. In trusts with extensive interests, separate persons may however be appointed, and in such cases the solicitor's duties include the negotiation of death duties and all legal work, while the factor is responsible for cash transactions, supervision of investments and preparation of trust accounts. If an executor or trustee acts in a professional capacity, e.g., as solicitor to the trust, no remuneration may be paid to him unless specifically authorised in the will (Lord Gray and Others, 1856, 19 D. 1, and Lewis' Trustees v. Pirie, 1912, S.C. 574). {Factor.}

A minute should be drawn by the solicitor for signature by the executors who accept office, giving him formal instructions and authority as to the administration of the estate. {First Minute of Executors.}

A

This may be in the following style :—

> First Minute of Meeting of the Executors of
> the late THOMAS SMITH held at 180 Princes
> Street, Edinburgh, on 11th December 1932.
>
> *Present :* Messrs John Smith, Albert
> Smith and John Williams, Executors ;
> and Mr T. Stewart of Messrs Williams
> & Stewart, W.S.

Mr Stewart reported that Mr Thomas Smith died in Edinburgh on
30th November 1932 and was buried at the Dean Cemetery, Edinburgh,
on 2nd December 1932. By his will dated 31st January 1929 and
codicil dated 24th August 1930 Mr Thomas Smith appointed Mrs Elizabeth
Smith, and Messrs John Smith, Albert Smith and John Williams to
be his executors. Mrs Elizabeth Smith predeceased him, and the other
executors accepted office.

The executors hereby appoint Messrs Williams & Stewart, W.S., to
be their solicitors and factors and instruct them :—

(1) To register the will in the Books of Council and Session.

(2) To ascertain the amount of the estate, and take possession of
securities and other documents.

(3) To advertise for claims against the estate, and pay the debts
and funeral expenses.

(4) To prepare an inventory of the estate, pay the estate duty
and take out confirmation.

(5) To complete the executors' title to the moveable estate.

(6) To intimate to the beneficiaries the bequests in the will.

(Executors sign here.)

Commencement of Administration. The solicitor is thus enabled to proceed with administration in the
following manner. He informs the executors as to the effect of the
will, stating the approximate amount of the estate so far as known,
and the will is at once registered in the Books of Council and Session
for preservation and an extract copy obtained there. Further extract
copies can be obtained at any time if required. Unless the unpaid
accounts are easily ascertained by correspondence, an advertisement is
inserted in the local newspapers instructing creditors to lodge claims
on the estate. All business papers belonging to deceased, including
titles to heritable property, share-certificates, bank pass-books, etc.,
are taken into the solicitor's possession, but delivery of documents
held by banks or other solicitors, etc., cannot legally be demanded
until the confirmation of executors has been completed, and they have
given the solicitor a written mandate.

The agent prepares the estate duty inventory which includes all
funds passing on the death, as explained in a separate chapter (see
page 125). The inventory is signed by one of the executors before a
Justice of the Peace or Notary Public, and lodged with the Estate Duty
Office within six months of date of death. If any additional estate is
discovered an additional or corrective inventory is required within two
months of the discovery.

After a preliminary scrutiny of the inventory by the Estate Duty Office it is returned with duty and interest assessed. Unless the proceeds of life policies can be made payable direct to the Inland Revenue, as is sometimes possible, none of deceased's estate is yet available for payment of the duty because the executors' title is not complete. Accordingly a temporary loan or overdraft is required, and in practice this is frequently obtained from the bank where deceased had an account, and secured by any balance at credit of that account, or deposit of investments, life policies or heritable titles, etc.

When the estate duty is paid, the inventory is sent to the Inland Revenue with the cheque, and the receipted inventory and the will are then lodged with the Sheriff Court (in Edinburgh the Commissary Court) of the Sheriffdom where deceased died domiciled. The Edinburgh Sheriff Court deals with Scottish estates where deceased died domiciled " furth of Scotland " or had no fixed domicile.

On payment of the dues of confirmation, the Sheriff, or in Edinburgh the Commissary Court, issues an official document known as the confirmation, which vests the moveable estate in Scotland in the executors. For each corrective inventory an eik (or additional confirmation) is issued, confirming the executors to the further estate, on payment of the additional duty, or if duty has been overpaid it is refunded or set off against legacy duty, etc. Additional copies or certified extracts from the confirmation may be obtained on payment of additional fees. The confirmation requires to be resealed at the Probate Courts in London or Belfast before it is effective as regards any estate in England or Northern Ireland, and for this purpose local agents are necessary to pay the dues there. Foreign and dominion estate requires special treatment, which is beyond the scope of this book. Before confirmation is obtained the solicitor should have informed the executors of the cash required to meet government duties and debts, etc., with a view to early realisation of such part of the estate as is necessary for payment of immediate liabilities. The executors decide how these will be met and which investments must first be realised. After confirmation is obtained, the executors' title to the estate is intimated by exhibition of the confirmation (or certified extracts) to bank-agents, secretaries of companies in which deceased had invested, and any others concerned. Fees for registration are usually charged by companies. At the same time the solicitor lodges dividend mandates signed by the executors authorising payment of future income to the bank or to himself on behalf of the executors. It is then possible to realise the estate, and bank balances are uplifted and investments realised as required.

Debts due by deceased are not payable until six months after date of death (Act of Sederunt, 1662). Claims lodged after the distribution of the estate fall on the executors personally if these are lodged before the expiry of the six months referred to, but not after that date, so executors are well advised to delay the final distribution until then. Creditors who hold security for their debts may realise the property secured, and account to the executors for any surplus. Certain debts are privileged and take preference over other creditors, and all ordinary creditors rank before legatees.

All available claims for recovery of income tax must be made by the executors as soon as possible, and they should also ascertain the total

Confirmation and Eik.

Payment of Debts.

amount of tax payable, by correspondence with the Inland Revenue authorities. Sur-tax is not payable until nine months after the close of the year of assessment. (See separate chapter on " Income Tax," page 39.)

Distribution
of Estate. All legacies and bequests of residue are subject to the prior legal rights of the surviving spouse and family of the deceased, explained in chapter on " Succession " (page 27). They must be informed of these rights and supplied with an estimate of the amount due, and they must then elect in writing either to accept the provisions of the will or to claim their legal rights.

Legacy or succession duty must be deducted from all legacies unless clearly declared in the will to be free of duty, and the duty is then payable to the Inland Revenue (see separate chapters, pages 130, 136). The appropriate forms must be lodged for assessment not later than twenty-one days after payment of the legacies.

The order of ranking of debts and legacies is as follows :—

(1) *Privileged Debts*—

Expenses of realisation and administration of the estate.
Deathbed expenses—restricted to suitable sums.
Funeral expenses—restricted similarly.
Mournings for family present at funeral—restricted similarly.
Wages of domestic and farm employees for current term.
Local rates for current year.
Income tax for any one year prior to death.
Note.—All the above rank equally.

(2) *Other debts* due by deceased.
(3) *Government duties.*
(4) *Legal rights* of surviving spouse and family.
(5) *Special legacies,* i.e., legacies of specified funds or articles.
(6) *General legacies,* i.e., legacies of fixed sums.
(7) *Residue of estate.*

The case of *Re* Pullen (1910, 1 Ch. 564) deals with the payment of debts where moveables are insufficient to meet these in full. If the estate is insufficient to pay all the debts and legacies the privileged debts form the first charge on the estate. Next, all the other debts due by deceased rank for payment, and so on. The following examples explain the " abating " of debts and legacies, that is, settling them by partial payments, in these circumstances.

Examples

I. *Insufficient Estate for Payment of Debts*—

Assuming estate of £200, privileged debts £20, and other debts £1800, the estate is divisible thus :—

Privileged debts	£20
Other debts 2s. per £1 on £1800 . .	180
	£200

There is nothing available for legatees.

II. *Insufficient Estate for Payment of Special Legacies*—

Assuming estate consisting of £1000 War Loan (worth say par), privileged debts £50, other debts £150, government duties £50, and two special legacies of £600 and £400 War Loan (=£1000 altogether), the estate is divisible thus :—

Privileged debts	£50
Other debts	150
Government duties	50
Cash requirements . . .	£250

The above sum is met by sale of £250 War Loan, leaving £750 stock for payment of the two legacies. They are then settled thus :

A. $\dfrac{750}{1000} \times £600 = £450$ War Loan

B. $\dfrac{750}{1000} \times £400 = £300$ War Loan

$£750$ War Loan

There is nothing available for general or residuary legatees.

III. *Insufficient Estate for Payment of General Legacies*—

Assuming estate of £3000 War Loan (worth say par) privileged debts £100, other debts £200, government duties £150, one special legacy of £1000 War Loan and three legacies (£1000, £500 and £500) £2000, with the residue to a charity specified, the estate is divisible thus :

Privileged debts	£100
Other debts	200
Government duties	150
	£450
Special legacy of £1000 War Loan . .	1000
	£1450

Legacy A. $\dfrac{1550}{2000} \times £1000$	. £775 0 0	
„ B. $\dfrac{1550}{2000} \times £500$.	. 387 10 0	
„ C. $\dfrac{1550}{2000} \times £500$.	. 387 10 0	
		1550
		£3000

In practice £2000 War Loan would probably be sold to pay the debts and general legacies, and the special legacy would be satisfied by transfer of £1000 War Loan. The charity gets nothing as there is no available residue.

A 2

Legacies are said to vest in the legatees when the right to the property belongs to them absolutely and indefeasibly, even although possession may be deferred until a later date. If the legatee's right has not vested and is dependent on circumstances, such as the attaining of a certain age, the legacy is known as contingent. Questions of vesting arising out of the interpretation of wills may involve very complicated points of law as to which it may be necessary to obtain judicial inter-pretation by way of " special case," in the courts. Actions of multiple-poinding are sometimes raised in order that all claiming to share in the funds of an executry or trust estate may have their respective rights determined by the court.

In terms of Act of Sederunt, dated 19th July 1934, Chapter IV., Rules 41-43, trustees may apply to the court for direction on questions relating to the investment, distribution, management or administration of the estate.

Legacy duty is payable on the residue of the estate, unless specifically exempted in the circumstances (see separate chapter, page 130). After a death duty clearance certificate has been obtained the executors may make a final distribution of the estate. The expenses of management are first ascertained and the solicitor's legal business account may be taxed by the Auditor of Court if desired by the executors. The executry accounts and scheme of division can then be completed and may be audited by the Accountant of Court or by an independent accountant appointed by the executors. Details of the procedure on division are given in separate chapters on " Schemes of Division " and " Audits " (pages 140, 147). If there is a continuing trust and the executors and trustees are different persons, the estate is transferred to the latter for subsequent administration by them. The executors are entitled to require receipts for any funds transferred by them to legatees or trustees, and these receipts should include approval of the accounts and acknowledgment of settlement of all claims. If the executors and trustees are the same persons the administration is then carried on as described below.

III. Trust Procedure

At the commencement of a trust unless it is merely a continuation of an executry the trustees should sign a formal minute appointing a solicitor and factor as in the following style :—

> First Minute of Trustees acting under the Ante-Nuptial Contract of Marriage between Mr John Jones and Miss Elizabeth Brown. *March* 1933.

First Minute of Trustees.

Messrs Williams & Stewart, W.S., intimated that Mr John Jones had instructed them to prepare an Ante-Nuptial Contract of Marriage between himself and Miss Elizabeth Brown. This has since been prepared, and after approval by both parties it was signed by them on 11th February 1933, and registered in the Books of Council and Session on 25th February 1933. In terms of the deed, Mr Jones assigned to Messrs James Williams, W.S., and Alexander Brown, C.A., as Trustees for purposes specified, £10,000 $3\frac{1}{2}$% War Loan for which a transfer has been prepared and is signed by the trustees along with this minute.

Mr Jones and Miss Brown were married at St Giles Cathedral, Edinburgh, on 11th February 1933.

The trustees hereby appoint Messrs Williams & Stewart, W.S., to be solicitors and factors in the trust and instruct them :—

(1) To retain in their possession the Extract Registered Ante-Nuptial Contract of Marriage.

(2) To register the said transfer of £10,000 $3\frac{1}{2}\%$ War Loan and retain the relative certificate.

(3) To prepare a mandate instructing the payment of interest on the War Loan to Mr Jones.

(Trustees sign here.)

After appointment the solicitor completes the trustees' title to the trust funds and prepares and lodges mandates instructing payment of the trust income to the beneficiaries or as may be otherwise arranged. A separate bank account may be opened by the trustees and any sums temporarily uninvested should be lodged on bank deposit. If the accounts may involve large sums, it is advisable that income be remitted direct to a bank account from which regular remittances may be made to the beneficiaries. Any surplus income which has been accumulated in terms of the trust disposition must be invested from time to time. **Completion of Title.**

Investments should be registered in the names of all the trustees, and in Scotland it is usual to add the words " Trustees of the late ——," but in England this registration is not accepted, and if any holdings are registered in the trustees' names as individuals they should sign an acknowledgment that they hold these securities for the trust.

If a local factor is appointed by the trustees in respect of heritable property, it is essential that he should render detailed statements of his transactions and remit the cash balance not less than once per annum, and the trust factor should audit these statements. It must be clearly arranged that only routine repairs may be ordered by the local factor, and any exceptional requirements should be reported to the trustees. **Local Factors.**

The respective rights of annuitants, liferenters and fiars are described in a separate chapter on " Liferent and Fee " (page 22). It may be noted that trust dispositions generally direct that the income is to be applied in one or more of the following ways for the benefit of specified beneficiaries :— **Income.**

(1) payment of life-annuities of fixed sums ;

(2) payments at the trustees' discretion to meet costs of maintenance and education, and accumulation of any surplus income until the occurrence of some specified event ;

(3) payment of the free income to the liferenters.

In order to make arrangements for the benefit of the liferenters and annuitants, an estimate of the annual income of the trust should be prepared by the factor. A conservative basis should be adopted, and allowances must be made for possible reductions in dividends, and changes in taxation, etc. As regards rents of heritable property a reserve is required for exceptional repairs, in addition to normal deductions in respect of annual charges and ordinary repairs. If apportionments are required (see separate chapter, page 46) these have the effect of diminishing the free income for the first year of the trust. Periodical remittances of income to the beneficiaries should be commenced as soon as possible.

Taxes and Death Duties. The factor must arrange for any income tax returns and claims which may be required. He should send all the beneficiaries annual certificates of their shares of the statutory income as computed for income tax purposes. The solicitor is responsible for negotiations as to any death duties which may fall due on the deaths of any of the annuitants or liferenters. (Separate chapters deal with income tax, estate duty, legacy duty and succession duty, pages 39, 114, 130, 136.)

Trust Accounts. The factor should prepare the trust accounts annually and submit them to the trustees and beneficiaries. If an audit by an independent accountant is required, the factor should send all the necessary documents to the auditor in order that he may be satisfied as to the accuracy of the accounts. If no independent audit is to be made the trustees should themselves examine all the documents.

Minute Book. For convenience, the factor should keep a sederunt book or minute book in which may be engrossed the will, confirmation, minutes of trustees' meetings, deeds of assumption and resignation of trustees, etc. Trust accounts may also be engrossed there, or, alternatively, may be placed in a permanent binding. A record of the births, marriages and deaths of the beneficiaries may conveniently be kept in the sederunt book.

Meetings of Trustees. The trustees should meet from time to time, and minutes of the meetings should be prepared by the solicitor, in which it is desirable to record fully all capital transactions. The trustees should approve of the trust accounts, and reconsider all the trust investments. Sometimes trustees' decisions may be made by correspondence, and in such cases formal minutes of trustees are desirable in order that the trust records may be complete. All minutes should be signed by every trustee. The procedure on changes in trustees by assumption and resignation is described later (page 11).

Discharge of Trustees. After completion of the trust purposes, the remaining funds may be divided among the beneficiaries entitled to share in the residue. (See chapter on "Schemes of Division," page 140.) They should be asked to sign a receipt and discharge, acknowledging full settlement of all claims against the trustees and discharging them from office.

Trustees may also be discharged on placing funds in court for distribution in terms of an action of multiple-poinding, or on petition to the court if no other discharge can be obtained (Trusts (Scotland) Act, 1921, sec. 18).

CHAPTER II

THE LAW OF TRUSTS

I. Scotland

In the following pages some of the principal points of the law as affecting trust accountancy are described. This chapter must be regarded merely as an introduction to the law of trusts.

The Trusts (Scotland) Act, 1921, governs all trusts constituted by deed, act of parliament, or royal charter, etc., and the common law of Scotland must also be kept in view.

The principal types of trusts are (a) *mortis causa* or testamentary trusts, constituted by the will of the testator, and (b) *inter vivos* trusts, constituted by deed of trust setting aside funds belonging to the truster during his lifetime. The latter type includes marriage-contract trusts, under either ante-nuptial or post-nuptial contracts of marriage. *(margin:* Constitution of Trusts.*)*

Under common law, trust purposes must not include any illegal act or be contrary to public policy or morals, and unless the purposes are clearly specified the trust may be void through uncertainty. Trusts for charitable or educational purposes may be continued in perpetuity, but restrictions on accumulations of any trust income were made by the Accumulations Act, 1800—known as the Thellusson Act. Under that act the period of accumulation is restricted (a) to the life of the truster in an *inter vivos* trust (see Stewart's Trustees *v.* Stewart, 1927, S.C. 350), and (b) in other trusts to the period expiring on the last of the following dates (1) the expiry of twenty-one years from the death of the truster, (2) the minority of any specified persons living at the date of his death, (3) the minority of any persons entitled to the accumulated trust income on attaining majority. In terms of the Trusts (Scotland) Act, 1921, sec. 9, a liferent of moveable estate may not be constituted in favour of persons unborn at the date of the deed. As regards successive liferents of heritage see Entail Amendment Act, 1848, sec. 48. *(margin:* Purposes of Trusts.*)*

The Trusts (Scotland) Act provides in secs. 10-15 as to authorised investments, and the principal classes of trustee securities are :— *(margin:* Authorised Investments.*)*

(1) U.K. government stocks, and stocks on which interest is guaranteed by parliament.
(2) Bank of England stock.
(3) Debenture stocks, debentures and mortgages of British railway companies.
(4) Preference and guaranteed, etc., stocks of British railway companies, on which the dividend is not contingent on profits, provided that any dividend (however small) has been paid on the ordinary stock of the company in question for each of the past ten years.
(5) Debentures, mortgages, bonds, or annuities, issued by muni-cipalities in Great Britain, Scottish local authorities, the

9

Metropolitan Water Board, etc., subject to certain conditions. (Sec. 10, subsecs. 6-8, 14, 15.)

(6) Indian government stocks.

(7) Feuduties and ground annuals.

(8) Loans on security of certain trustee investments.

(9) Loans on security of heritable property in Great Britain.

(10) Indian railway stocks, etc., on which the interest is guaranteed by the Indian government and payable in sterling.

(11) Purchase or loans on security of stocks approved by the court. By Act of Sederunt, dated 18th March 1926, the Court of Session has authorised trustees to invest in preference stocks of any British railway company, even if dividends are contingent on profits, if dividends of at least 3% have been paid on the ordinary stock of the company for each of the past ten years.

(12) Stocks registered under the Colonial Stock Acts, *i.e.*, issued by governments of the British Dominions, provided that the price paid is (*a*) not over redemption value if the stock may be redeemed within fifteen years, or (*b*) not over 15% over redemption value in other cases.

In terms of sec. 33 a trustee is not to be liable for breach of trust because an investment has been retained which has ceased to be an authorised investment. Trustees must not hold bearer securities beyond the time required for realisation or conversion into registered or inscribed form (sec. 15). If wider powers of investment are given by the trust disposition the Trusts (Scotland) Act is not to be held as restricting them to those referred to above, which powers are, however, implied in all trusts as a minimum unless specifically prohibited (secs. 10, 11, 14). Unauthorised investments should be sold as soon as possible, and any available capital balances should be invested in securities authorised by the Trusts (Scotland) Act and the trust disposition.

Heritable Bonds.

If it is proposed to lend any part of the trust funds on bond and disposition in security over heritable property, a valuation of the property must be made by an independent valuer, and the loan must not exceed two-thirds of the stated value. (Trusts (Scotland) Act, sec. 30.) On making such a loan the trustees' rights as heritable creditors should be intimated to the insurance company which has insured the property against fire.

Trustees' Powers.

The Trusts (Scotland) Act, 1921, sec. 4, gives powers to trustees *inter alia* to do the following acts unless they are at variance with the trust disposition :—

(1) Sell the trust estate.

(2) Borrow money on security of the trust funds.

(3) Appoint factors and law-agents and pay them suitable remuneration. No remuneration may be paid to trustees either directly or indirectly, unless specifically authorised (see page 1).

(4) Discharge trustees who have resigned and the representatives of those who have died.

On a petition to the court by trustees the court may, if it is considered expedient, grant certain powers (including the above powers) even if these are at variance with the terms of the trust (sec. 5).

Unless the contrary is expressed, a quorum of trustees is constituted by a majority of those accepting and surviving, and such a quorum has full powers to act without the minority (sec. 3 and sec. 7). Other points of importance in the Trusts (Scotland) Act as to the trustees' powers are (1) the court may in certain circumstances authorise trustees to advance capital to beneficiaries not of age, unless prohibited by the trust disposition (sec. 16), and (2) trustees may apply to the court for audit of their accounts by the Accountant of Court (sec. 17).

Sec. 3 provides that unless the contrary is expressed all trusts include power to trustees to assume additional trustees, or to resign, except (1) in the case of a sole trustee who cannot resign until new trustees or a judicial factor have been appointed, and (2) trustees who have received legacies, annuities, etc., given on condition of accepting office, who cannot resign unless this is expressly authorised, or if permission is granted by the court. Secs. 19 and 20 describe the procedure on resignation. If trustees cannot be assumed in terms of a trust deed the court may appoint one or more trustees (sec. 22). *Assumption and Resignation of Trustees.*

A deed of assumption which includes a general conveyance is effective in conveying to the new trustees all Scots estate—both heritable and moveable. If owing to the absence or incapacity of a trustee the necessary quorum of trustees cannot be obtained for such a deed, the court may grant consent to the assumption (secs. 3 and 21). In order that full effect may be given to a deed of assumption and/or resignation it must be recorded in the Books of Council and Session, and the extract registered with all companies in which the trustees have invested. Investments registered in the trustees' individual names (not described as trustees) require transfer on common form from the whole old trustees to the whole new trustees, with a 10s. stamp on each transfer.

If a sole trustee dies or is incapable of acting in the trust, any person who is entitled absolutely to any trust property may apply to the court for authority to complete his own title to the property, and the court may grant this authority (sec. 24). If no one is so entitled, the executors of a deceased sole trustee may complete their title to the trust property, but only in order immediately to transfer it to a judicial factor, the heir-in-heritage, beneficiaries, or persons authorised by the trust disposition to make the appointment of a new trustee. The court may appoint trustees in place of a sole trustee who has been absent from the U.K. for six months, or is insane or otherwise incapable of acting (sec. 22). It is always preferable that at least two trustees should act in all trusts in order to prevent delay and difficulties which inevitably arise on the death or incapacity of a sole trustee.

If a sole trustee desires to resign he may first assume additional trustees, or if this is impracticable he must apply to the court for appointment of trustees or a judicial factor (secs. 3 and 19).

On the death of any trustee the death certificate should be registered with all companies in which investments are held by the trustees.

Trustees may be removed by the court if (1) insane, (2) incapable either physically or mentally, or (3) absent for more than six months from the United Kingdom or having disappeared for a like period (sec. 23). Under common law the court may remove a trustee for breach of trust, or obstructing the administration, or where he is proved to have endangered the trust property.

Responsibility of Trustees. Trustees become personally liable to the beneficiaries for any losses arising through their negligence or breach of trust (Town and County Bank v. Walker, 1904, 12, S.L.T. 411). It has been said that a trustee must use the same diligence that a man of ordinary prudence would exercise in his own affairs (Raes v. Meek, 1889, 16 R. (H.L.) 31). Under common law a trustee must not be *Auctor in Rem Suam*, that is, his duty as trustee must not conflict with his personal interest. Arising from this, trustees must not receive any financial reward for their services, nor receive loans from the trust funds, nor purchase any of the trust property, unless any of these are specifically authorised in the trust disposition. Another important rule of common law is that profits arising from unauthorised investments or from other breaches of trust belong to the trust, despite the fact that losses must be made up by the trustees as noted above.

There have been many court cases on questions arising out of trust administration and the following decisions are considered to be of special importance. In Speight v. Gaunt (1883, 9 A.C. 1) it was held that trustees cannot delegate their supervisory powers which are essentially personal, but they may employ skilled assistance, and in certain circumstances this may, in fact, be a duty. Agents must, however, be appointed and supervised with prudence and must not be left in control of large sums. In *Re* Hotham (1902, 2 Ch. 575) it was decided that new investments must be carefully considered, including even any trustee investments which might in certain circumstances be undesirable. The case of Ross v. Ross (1896, 23 R. (H.L.) 67) decided that proper accounts must be kept and exhibited to the beneficiaries. In Clarke v. Clarke's Trustees (1925, S.C. 693) it was held that (1) investments must be reconsidered by the trustees from time to time with a view to selling any of them which cannot wisely be retained, and (2) capital must not be retained uninvested whether in cash or on bank deposit, and if this is done the trustees may be liable to make up the income to the amount which should have been earned.

Indemnity. Sec. 3 grants an indemnity to trustees to the extent that unless the contrary is expressed they are liable only for their own acts and not liable for acts of their co-trustees nor for omissions. It must be noted, however, that neither this section nor an indemnity clause in a trust disposition protects trustees who have acted negligently (Ferguson v. Paterson, 1900, 2 F., H.L. 37).

For further details of the law of trusts, readers are referred to the Trusts (Scotland) Act, 1921. Separate chapters of this book describe the principal points of the law as to judicial factories, succession, liferent and fee, income tax, death duties and apportionments.

II. COMPARISONS BETWEEN SCOTS AND ENGLISH TRUST LAW

It is not within the scope of this book to deal adequately with the differences in trust law and practice as between Scotland and England, but in the following pages a brief survey of this subject has been attempted. The law of trusts in England is based on the Trustee Act,

1925, which is in many respects similar to the Trusts (Scotland) Act, 1921, although the former is more comprehensive.

Trustees' statutory powers of investment in Scotland and England are different in various respects. For example, in England trustees may invest in the following, which are not authorised in Scotland :— Powers of Investment.

(1) Bank of Ireland stock.
(2) Certain Indian railway company annuities.
(3) Stocks issued by authorised water commissioners with power to levy rates over an area with a population of at least 50,000.

British railway debenture stocks are only fully authorised English trustee investments if 3% dividend has been paid on the ordinary stock of the company for each of the past ten years, while in Scotland these debenture stocks retain full status irrespective of ordinary dividend rates. Similarly railway preference and guaranteed stocks are only authorised by the English Trustee Act if 3% has been paid on the ordinary stock for each of the past ten years, while in Scotland so long as any dividend has been paid on the ordinary stock for that period the trustee status of the prior stocks is unaffected. But additional securities approved by order of the English courts (known as the Chancery List) at present include debenture, preference, and guaranteed, etc., stocks of British railway companies which have paid a dividend on their ordinary stocks for each of the past ten years. Bearer securities are permitted as authorised investments in England, unless specifically prohibited in the will, if the registered stock of the same issue is authorised, but they must be deposited with a bank (Trustee Act, sec. 7). No such powers are given in Scotland (Trusts (Scotland) Act, sec. 15). Restrictions on purchases of certain stocks at a premium in England are made by Trustee Act, sec. 2, and these have no parallel in Scotland except as regards stocks issued under the Colonial Stock Acts (Trusts (Scotland) Act, sec. 11).

The Trustee Act, sec. 10 (3), gives power to trustees to concur in schemes of arrangement for reconstruction, etc., of companies in which they are interested, and sec. 10 (4) deals with rights to new shares, but there are no similar statutory provisions in Scotland. There is another interesting difference as regards audits which in England are not normally required more than once every three years (Trustee Act, sec. 22 (4)). In Scotland trustees have common law powers which are similar to this section, but annual audits are usual. Powers of Trustees.

Advances to contingent beneficiaries in respect of capital are permitted in England at the trustees' discretion under certain restrictions (Trustee Act, sec. 32), while in Scotland it is necessary to obtain court authority for these payments (Trusts (Scotland) Act, sec. 16).

In Scotland there are no restrictions as to the number of trustees, and one trustee may legally act alone, but in England in certain circumstances not more than four nor fewer than two trustees are required (Trustee Act, secs. 14, 34, 37). Provision is made by English law for a trustee who is temporarily abroad delegating his powers by power of attorney (Trustee Act, sec. 25), but in Scotland no delegation is permissible. A majority in Scotland may, however, act without the minority (secs. 3 (c) and 7) which is not allowed in England, where in general all trustees must concur in any decision. Changes in Trustees.

In England if a sole trustee has died new trustees can be appointed by deed signed by his personal representatives (Trustee Act, sec. 36), whereas in Scotland an application to the court would usually be required in those circumstances. Other differences in procedure as to changes in trustees may be observed on comparison of Trustee Act, sec. 36, with Trusts (Scotland) Act, secs. 19-23. It is important to note that in England trustees who are absent from the U.K. for over twelve months, or who are unfit or refuse to act as trustees, may be removed from office by their co-trustees or certain other persons. In Scotland in such circumstances an application to the court is required, but the limit for absence from the U.K. is only six months.

Executors. An administrator under general grant of administration in England is similar to an executor-dative in Scotland, *e.g.*, where there is a will but no executor is appointed, or none has accepted office. In certain circumstances the court grants only limited powers to an administrator under " special grant " in England, which has no parallel in Scotland.

Probate in England corresponds generally with confirmation in Scotland, but neither is effective as regards investments in the other country until the deed has been resealed by the court there, although this is merely a formality. The English probate act is usually known as the probate, *i.e.*, the document authorising the executors to realise the estate, and this consists of a copy of the will with an official seal attached. The Scots confirmation gives the names of executors, etc., and also details the whole moveable estate in Great Britain.

Executors and administrators in England are known as the legal personal representatives of the deceased, but this term is not used in Scotland.

Intestacy. The Administration of Estates Act, 1925, details the powers of an administrator in an intestacy in England and gives the basis of division of such estates, which may be summarised thus :—

(1) Personal chattels, that is motor-cars, horses, furniture, jewellery, etc., pass to the surviving husband or wife, who also receives the first £1000 with 5% interest from date of death.

(2) Residue of estate falls to children, subject to liferent by surviving spouse of one-half thereof, but if any children are under twenty-one years of age and are unmarried, their rights are not vested until the earlier of these two events. Children of predeceasing children rank *per stirpes*.

(3) If no children survive, the whole residue is liferented by the surviving spouse passing on his or her death to the next-of-kin, *i.e.*, parents, whom failing brothers and sisters, etc.

Details of intestate succession in Scotland are given in chapter on " Succession " (page 31).

Legal Rights. There are no legal rights of relatives in England, so that a man may leave all his property to any person, but in Scotland a surviving spouse and children have rights which cannot be defeated by the will.

Apportionments. Contrary to Scots law, apportionments are not required on purchases and sales of investments during a liferent in England, but if a dividend has recently been declared on an investment bought " cum. div." the dividend is applicable to capital. (See *Re* Sir Robert Peel's Estates, 1910, 1 Ch. 389.)

Under English law equitable apportionments may arise in certain circumstances, unless apparently excluded by the will. For example, under Howe *v.* Earl of Dartmouth (1802, 7 Ves. 147) the income on unauthorised investments or wasting assets, etc., is all applicable to capital, and the lifetenant is entitled only to the rate earned on trustee investments. The principle of equitable apportionment is not often applicable in Scotland.

The Public Trustee in England has no parallel in Scotland. His Official powers are stated in the Public Trustee Act, 1906, Public Trustee Rules, Supervision. 1912, and Judicature Act, 1925, sec. 175 (1), and include the audit of trust accounts, in addition to the administration of trusts, in which he can act either solely or along with other trustees. The Trusts (Scotland) Act, however, gives power to trustees to place the administration under court supervision by annual audit by the Accountant of Court (sec. 17). The law of Scotland also gives power to the court to appoint judicial factors to administer trusts where there are no trustees surviving, and in certain other circumstances. A judicial factor is usually, although not necessarily, an accountant or solicitor. (See separate chapter, page 16.)

The style of trust accounts is different in Scotland and England, as explained in chapter on " Preparation of Trust Accounts " (page 71).

A lifetenant in England is comparable with a liferenter in Scotland, and a remainderman, similarly, with a fiar. Other legal terms which are dissimilar will be found in other chapters of this book.

CHAPTER III

JUDICIAL FACTORIES

I. Introduction

JUDICIAL factors may be appointed by the court to administer specified funds under superintendence of the Accountant of Court so as to protect the interests of all those entitled to share in them. The following acts govern the appointment and powers of such factors :—Judicial Factors (Scotland) Acts, 1849, 1880 and 1889 ; Guardianship of Infants Acts, 1886 and 1925 ; Bankruptcy (Scotland) Act, 1913 ; Trusts (Scotland) Act, 1921 ; and Act of Sederunt dated 19th July 1934, Chapter I., Rules 41-44, and Chapter IV., Rules 11-13.

Definition.   A judicial factor is any person judicially appointed factor, either on the estate of a person who is legally incapable of managing his own affairs, or on a trust estate, and also includes guardians where caution is required. See Trusts (Scotland) Act, sec. 2, and Act of Sederunt, dated 19th July 1934, Chapter IV., Rule 11.

Circumstances of Appointment and Discharge.   The principal types of judicial factories are as follows :—

(1) *Factor loco tutoris* appointed on behalf of a pupil (*i.e.*, a boy under fourteen or a girl under twelve years of age), if the pupil is in Scotland or has property there. On the pupil attaining minority the factor automatically becomes *curator bonis* (1889 Act, sec. 11).

(2) *Curator bonis to minor* appointed in similar circumstances on behalf of a child who is under twenty-one but over fourteen years of age (or twelve if a girl). The appointment requires the minor's consent. On the attaining of majority the funds may be paid over to the ward and the factor then petitions for discharge.

(3) *Curator bonis to incapax* appointed on behalf of a person who is physically or mentally incapable of managing his own affairs, if no legal guardian is available. The incapacity must be certified by two medical practitioners by holograph writing, and the incapax must be either domiciled or resident in Scotland or possessing property there. If the ward recovers from his incapacity the funds may be paid over to him, and the factor then petitions for discharge.

(4) *Factor loco absentis* appointed on behalf of a person who is missing but who is believed to be alive, and who has rights or property in Scotland of which he is believed to be ignorant. If the ward returns, or appoints an agent to act for him, the funds may be paid over as instructed by him, and the factor then petitions for discharge.

(5) *Factor on a trust estate.*—The appointment may be made on lapse of trustees, *e.g.*, (*a*) if no trustees were named in the will, (*b*) if

those named have declined office, (c) if those named have predeceased the testator, (d) if all the original trustees have died without assuming others to act along with them, (e) if the trustees are removed by the court.

The appointment may also be made (a) where there is a deadlock in administration owing to disputes among the trustees, or (b) in respect of the estate of any person who has died intestate.

In all these cases the factor cannot be discharged until the estate has been wholly distributed on completion of the trust, or until another factor is appointed in his place. Such an appointment is made by the court on a petition for discharge of the former factor and appointment of a new factor.

In these circumstances discharge is not granted until the whole estate has been transferred to the latter.

(6) *Factor on a deceased's estate under the Bankruptcy (Scotland) Act, 1913, sec. 163.*—The appointment is made where no trustees have been appointed or none accepts office, on the petition of a creditor or successor, and the factor must administer the estate and divide the funds in accordance with the rules of the Bankruptcy Act.

(7) *Factors under Act of Sederunt of 19th July 1934.*—The appointment is made for the administration of sums of damages awarded by the court to minors and pupils, in terms of Chapter I., Rules 41-44, of the Act of Sederunt. The court must be satisfied either (1) that no person is available to give a full and valid discharge for such sum, or (2) that the administration of the sum for the benefit of the child cannot otherwise be reasonably secured.

II. NOTES AS TO FACTORIES, TYPES 1-5 (ABOVE)

The appointment is made by the court on a petition by any person Appointment interested in the preservation of the funds in question, such as trustees, creditors, or heirs. A petition may be lodged by an incapax for appointment of a judicial factor on his own estate, although this is unusual. The Lord Advocate may petition for the appointment of a judicial factor on a charitable trust or on the estate of an incapax, and the Accountant of Court may also petition in the latter case. The Sheriff may make the appointment (1) if the annual income is under £100, or (2) if the petition is under the Bankruptcy Act and the total assets do not exceed £500. Otherwise the Court of Session must make the appointment.

The person on whose estate the factor acts is known as his ward.

Caution is required to be found by the factor in terms of 1849 Act, secs. 2 and 27, and may be granted by an individual giving his personal guarantee, or by an approved guarantee association. A bond of caution is signed by the cautioner, who thus becomes a surety (or guarantor) against loss through default by the factor.

Premiums on guarantee bonds may generally be charged in the judicial factor's accounts. It is necessary that the bond of caution should be lodged with the Accountant of Court within three weeks of

B

the appointment in cases under the Sheriff's jurisdiction or appointments under the Bankruptcy Act, but one month is allowed in other cases. Additional caution may be required by the Accountant of Court during the subsistence of a factory, or reduction may be allowed. (See Act of Sederunt, Chapter IV., Rule 12.)

Completion of Title.

An extract act and decree of the court appointing the judicial factor is obtained, and after this is stamped by the Inland Revenue it constitutes the factor's authority to complete his title. Exemptions from stamp duty are conferred in cases of factors *loco absentis*, or *loco tutoris*, and in any estates which are wholly heritable, but where special powers to make up title are granted this exemption does not apply. Stamping of the extract must be effected within thirty days of extracting the original act and decree. The factor's title to heritable property in Scotland is completed by recording the act and decree in the register of sasines, and his title to investments by registering it with the companies concerned. (See Judicial Factors Act, 1889, F.A. 1916, sec. 66, and Railways Act, 1921.)

Inventory.

A printed form is supplied by the Accountant of Court on which is prepared an inventory of the whole estate as at the date of the appointment of the factor, which must be lodged with the Accountant within six months (1849 Act, sec. 3). In addition to details of the funds the annual income is shown, and particulars are required as to the age of the ward, and the caution which has been found. The Accountant of Court requires for perusal all share certificates, titles to heritable properties, valuations of furniture, certified bank pass-books, etc., in order to vouch the inventory, and no realisations should be made before these have been examined by him.

Notes on subsequent administration of judicial factories are given below (Sec. V.). As regards the distribution of the funds if the estate is insolvent, a statement of funds and scheme of division may be required by the court before the distribution is made, as if the factor was appointed under the Bankruptcy Act (Act of Sederunt, 19th July 1934, Chapter IV., Rule 12 *h*).

If the ward dies, the factor pays over the estate to the executors on exhibition of confirmation in their favour.

After the final account has been prepared showing the distribution of the estate, it is audited by the Accountant of Court. The printed instructions for the guidance of judicial factors give full particulars of his requirements in this connection. The discharge of a judicial factor may be granted on petition to the court, but cannot be obtained until the final account has been audited.

III. Notes as to Bankruptcy Act Factories

The following notes summarise the principal points of procedure in terms of the Act of Sederunt of 19th July 1934, Chapter IV., Rule 13. Within seven days of extracting his appointment, a notice calling for claims must be inserted by the factor in the *Edinburgh Gazette*, and in such newspapers as he thinks proper. The notice should be in the form No. 23 prescribed in the Act of Sederunt, and a copy of that *Gazette* must be lodged in process. The factor then examines the claims and ranks them for payment, treating the date of his appointment as equivalent to the date of sequestration. Caution is necessary as noted above, and the usual inventory of the estate is required within six months of appointment, and there is also required to be lodged a detailed statement of the creditors' and successors' claims against the estate.

Interim distributions may be made to the creditors after six months from date of death of the deceased, at the factor's discretion, subject however to examination of the scheme of division by the Accountant of Court, and approval by the court. Deathbed and funeral expenses, and other preferential claims, may be paid before the expiry of six months if sufficient funds are available.

After the whole estate is realised, a state of funds and scheme of division must be lodged with the Accountant of Court. After his report thereon has been completed the factor lodges it in court, and must intimate this to each creditor individually, also by notice in the *Edinburgh Gazette* (Form No. 24). Each creditor must be informed of the amount for which he has been ranked and the proposed dividend due to him. Any persons interested in the distribution may lodge objections to the proposed division within three weeks, and the court hears counsel for the objectors and for the factor, before approving of the scheme either with or without amendment.

Any surplus estate, after payment of the creditors, must be reported to the Accountant of Court, and may be paid over to those claiming to be successors, or retained by the factor, under the directions of the court. When the factor has distributed the whole funds and wishes to petition for discharge, he must serve the petition on the representatives of the deceased and on his cautioner, and also insert a notice in the *Edinburgh Gazette* (Form No. 25). The petition will not be disposed of by the court until the expiry of fourteen days after such service and notice, nor until formal acceptances of service of the petition and a copy of that *Gazette* are lodged in process.

IV. NOTES AS TO FACTORIES UNDER 1934 ACT *re* DAMAGES AWARDED TO MINORS AND PUPILS

The procedure is simplified and the factor's duties are more or less restricted to dealing with the sum awarded by order of court, although the court may grant him additional powers in his ward's interest. Application for the appointment is by motion within seven days of the court decree and this may be enrolled by any party to the action. After appointment the factor must find caution and obtain an extract of his appointment.

When the factor's duties are completed his application for discharge is made by letter to the Principal Clerk of Session, who, with concurrence of the Accountant of Court, may bring the application before the Lord Ordinary sitting in Chambers. Appointments on the factor's death or resignation may be effected similarly.

V. ADMINISTRATION OF JUDICIAL FACTORIES

A separate bank account should be opened for each judicial factory, and all cash received should be paid into this account (1849 Act, sec. 5). The amount of cash in hands of the factor must not exceed £50 for over

Cash Transactions

ten days, and in Sheriff Court factories is restricted to £25 for that period.

Intimations
of Changes.
Changes such as the death or insolvency of a cautioner, recovery of ward from incapacity, or death of the factor, ward or other beneficiary, should be reported to the Accountant of Court at once.

On death of a factor, a petition for appointment of a new factor may be lodged in court by any persons interested in the estate, or the Accountant of Court may submit a report to the court to the same effect. The executors of the deceased factor must account to the new factor for the whole funds of the factory (1889 Act, sec. 10).

Factor's
Powers and
Duties.
All documents relating to the factory must be taken into the factor's possession as soon as possible after his appointment. Any sums which are due to the estate should be collected and all unauthorised investments must be sold. The funds may require to be distributed immediately, but if there is a continuing trust the whole available funds should be invested in authorised trustee investments. Investments in English companies should be registered in the name of the judicial factor as an individual, as trusts are not generally recognised by them, but in this connection a letter acknowledging the trust or an endorsement by the factor on the certificates is required for audit purposes.

The powers of judicial factors are in general similar to the powers of trustees, but a judicial factor cannot resign his office without the authority of the court and cannot assume trustees to act with him (Trusts (Scotland) Act, sec. 3). Before entering into legal proceedings a report of the circumstances should be made to the Accountant of Court whose approval is required. Special powers may be granted by the court on petition, and such petitions should first be submitted to the Accountant (1849 Act, sec. 7). A case dealing with the powers of judicial factors in completing title to heritage is Annan—Leslie's Factor, 1925, S.C. 464. If a factor is negligent he may be fined and removed from office by the court (1849 Act, sec. 6).

Accounts.
Except as regards the first account, when the period of the account may be fixed by the Accountant of Court as between six and eighteen months, accounts are required by the Accountant of Court annually and these must be prepared in the prescribed form as shown in the printed instructions issued by him. A note as to income tax recovered should be inserted stating to what date claims have been made, and an account current and rental are shown in addition to the usual form of account charge and discharge. If any additional estate has been discovered full particulars must be stated (1849 Act, sec. 3). A docquet must be appended stating whether or not feuduty receipts and adequate fire insurance premium receipts have been seen in respect of all heritable property over which bonds and dispositions in security are held. Such bonds should be first bonds and preferably not in excess of one-half of the value of the property.

Factor's Re-
muneration.
The Accountant of Court fixes the remuneration of the factor on a commission basis each year at the time of the audit, and no charge should be made in the first account—each year's commission appearing in the next account. Legal business accounts incurred by the factor must be taxed by the Auditor of the Court of Session or Sheriff Court.

Audit.
After completion of the account it must be signed by the factor and lodged with vouchers for audit by the Accountant of Court usually

within one month of the end of the period (1849 Act, sec. 4), although in special circumstances an additional period of two months is allowed. Securities are examined later when requested by the Accountant. In connection with heritable bonds, a solicitor's certificate of ranking of the bonds, a valuation of the property, and a certificate by the Assessor as to its rental, are all required at the first audit. Notes may be issued by the Accountant of Court along with his draft report for answer and comment by the factor, and when these notes have been satisfactorily answered the Accountant issues his note of audit fee, but the factor does not receive the report.

CHAPTER IV

LIFERENT AND FEE

Liferenter and Fiar.

A LIFERENTER (fem. liferentrix) is any person entitled to the liferent of property, that is, its use and enjoyment without destruction of the corpus or capital.

A fiar is any person entitled to the fee or absolute ownership of property, although simultaneously a liferent may exist in favour of another person, in which case the fiar's interest is restricted accordingly.

In general, capital belongs to the fiar and income to the liferenter, and the trustees of property which is subject to liferent must always keep this in view and act in the best interests of both. There is, of course, to some extent a conflict of interests between liferenter and fiar.

Alimentary Liferents.

Alimentary liferents are not assignable, that is, the liferenter cannot transfer his right to another person. Such liferents also cannot be attached by creditors for payment of the liferenter's debts, and they are not brought to an end if the liferenter also becomes fiar, nor can they be discharged by the liferenter. In non-alimentary liferented trusts the trust may be wound up and the funds transferred to the fiar, if liferent and fee are vested in the same person. (See Miller's Trustees *v.* Miller, 1890, 18 R. 301 and Main's Trustees *v.* Main, 1917, S.C. 660, as to the right of a fiar to bring a trust to an end.)

Liferents may be granted for the whole life of the beneficiary or for a specified shorter period, for example, until marriage. Liferenters may assign their rights, unless declared to be alimentary, but this does not affect the period of the liferent.

Legal and Conventional Liferents.

Liferents may arise (*a*) through operation of the legal rights of terce and courtesy, or (*b*) by creation under deed or agreement. The former are known as legal liferents and the latter as conventional liferents.

Formerly, deeds sometimes created direct liferents, that is, the property continued to be owned personally by the grantor of the deed and no trustees were appointed, but this is now unusual. These direct or " proper " liferents were either " by constitution " in favour of another person, but reserving the fee to the grantor, or—the converse— " by reservation " where the liferent was reserved to the grantor, but the fee was conveyed to another.

The usual form of liferent is now the indirect or " beneficiary " liferent where trustees are appointed in the deed which creates it. These trustees hold the property until the expiry of the liferent when it is conveyed to the fiar.

Capital and Income.

In practice it is important to keep in view the distinction between capital and income in the various transactions of the trust, and as explained in a separate chapter (page 46) it is sometimes necessary to make apportionments of rents, dividends and burdens on property, which are *prima facie* applicable to income.

In testamentary trusts the original capital consists of all property

22

owned by deceased at his death, subject to deduction of debts payable, and deathbed and funeral expenses. In other trusts the capital at the beginning is made up of the whole funds placed in trust.

Debts due by deceased include tradesmen's accounts, wages, income tax to date of death, and a proportion of current year's rent, rates, feuduty and bond-interest, etc. Debts in respect of deceased's wife and family, who were maintained by him, are included if incurred prior to the date of death.

Deathbed and funeral expenses consist of nursing home and doctors' fees, undertaker's account, price of ground in cemetery, and tombstone.

Additions to the capital of the trust may arise owing to the receipt of legacies and gifts, or increases on realisation of investments over the value when received or purchased by the trustees. Deductions from capital include government duties, legacies, management expenses, and decreases on realisation of investments.

There are many points in the allocation of transactions between capital and income which require further consideration and some of these are now described.

I. *Heritable Properties :—*

Farm stocks must be maintained approximately in the same state throughout the " life " of the trust. (See Rogers, 1867, 5, M. 1078.) Timber on the estate is part of the capital, but ordinary windfalls and mature coppice wood may be used by the liferenter, who is also entitled to sufficient wood for maintenance of buildings and fences, etc., on the estate. (See Dickson, 1823, 2, S. 152 (N.E. 138).)

Difficulties may arise as to proceeds of minerals found on the estate, but usually there are specific instructions in the trust disposition. If no directions are given the liferenter is entitled to minerals required for the estate and also to profits from mineral rights let by the testator, but not profits arising from mineral leases created by the trustees. (See Campbell v. Wardlaw, 1883, 10 R., H.L. 65.)

Improvements to heritable property are chargeable to capital as additional investments in the property. Restoration of property which has fallen into decay is an " improvement."

Annual payments such as repairs, rates and taxes, bond-interest, minister's stipend, teind, ground-annual and feuduty are payable out of income. Fire insurance premiums, etc., must also be charged wholly to income. (Glover's Trustees v. Glover, 1913, S.C. 115.)

II. *Investments :—*

Where heritable bonds carrying arrears of interest are realised at a loss, it is necessary to allocate the proceeds between capital and income. The leading case is Dempster's Trustees v. Dempster (1898, 35, S.L.R. 657). Under this decision the sum applicable to capital is the amount which, if invested at a reasonable rate of interest (compounded annually) as from the date to which interest was paid in full, would have produced the actual sum received. If arrears of interest began before the testator's death the latter date is taken instead of the former for the calculation.

The total proceeds for this purpose include any surplus rents over expenses, during the period when the bondholder was in possession of the property, pending sale.

Thus, if a bondholder p. £2000 at 5% was in possession of a property for two years and then sold the property the apportionment is as follows :—

Total rents for two years (say) . . .		£200
Proceeds of sale (say)		1500
		£1700
Less Two years' rates, etc. (say)	£120	
Expenses of sale (say) .	25	
		145
Net total proceeds		£1555

The sum which would produce £1555 in two years at say 5% compound interest is made up thus :—

$$\text{£}\frac{1555}{(1\cdot05)^2} \;=\; \text{£}\frac{1555}{1\cdot1025} \;=\; \text{£}1410 \quad 8 \quad 7$$

This calculation can be proved by calculating the interest on this sum, thus :—

Interest at 5% (first year) on £1410, 8s. 7d.	£70	10	5
Interest at 5% (second year) on £1480, 19s. (£1410, 8s. 7d.+ £70, 10s. 5d.)	74	1	0
	144	11	5
	£1555	0	0

The sum of £1555 is therefore allocated £1410, 8s. 7d. to capital and £144, 11s. 5d. to income.

A question not free from doubt arises on purchases of redeemable investments at a price in excess of the redemption price. It is prudent to write off this premium against income during the " life " of the investment, but there is no general rule of law which authorises this. (See Heath v. Baxter's Trustees, 1902, 10, S.L.T. 462.)

Bonus shares and cash bonuses may be applicable to capital or income, depending on whether or not they are issued from profits which have been capitalised. Even if the company had no power to capitalise the profits, they might be deemed to have been capitalised if the accumulations had in fact been used as part of the capital. (See Irving v. Houston, 1803, 4 Paton, S.C. App. 521, and Bouch v. Sproule, 1887, 12, A.C. 385.)

The deciding factor is the primary intention of the company as expressed or implied, in respect of capitalisation—thus a regular

dividend in shares would probably be treated as income, while a
bonus described as " a capital bonus of 1 share for every 3 held "
would be applicable to capital. Leading cases on this subject are
Bouch v. Sproule, 1887, 12, A.C. 385 ; re Alsbury, 1890, 45, Ch.D.
237 ; Cunliffe's Trustees v. Cunliffe, 1900, 3, F. 202 ; Howard's
Trustees v. Howard, 1907, S.C. 1274 ; Inland Revenue v. Blott,
1921, 2, A.C. 171 ; and Inland Revenue v. Fisher, 1926, A.C. 395.

Proceeds of sales of rights to new shares are applicable to capital,
but discount on prepayment of calls on new issues is income.

Arrears of dividends should be apportioned over the period in
respect of which they are declared and not the period when the
profits were earned. The English case of Wakley v. Vachell (1920,
2, Ch. 205) appears to be inconsistent with the Apportionment Act
and would probably not be followed in Scotland. (This case decided
that when arrears of dividends were received, these were applicable
to the years in which they were earned, despite the terms of the
resolution declaring the dividends to be in respect of previous years
when no profits were earned.)

III. *Annuities :—*

An annuity is a right to receive a fixed sum each year for a
specified number of years, or until the occurrence of a stated event,
or in perpetuity. In trusts, annuities are frequently payable either
for life or until marriage of the annuitant. While annuities are
primarily charges against income, they are payable whether or not
there is sufficient income unless the contrary is stated. (Kinmond's
Trustees v. Kinmond, 1873, 11, M. 381.)

Sometimes other provision is made for dealing with deficiencies
of income, for example, by deferring the date of payment until
income is available, or by restricting the annuities to the actual
free income. (The latter is really a restricted liferent with a
maximum limit.)

In practice therefore the annuities are chargeable to income,
but generally subject to a transfer from capital account to meet
any deficiency.

IV. *Legal and Management Expenses :—*

These expenses are divisible between capital and income
according to the general nature of the work. Thus capital account
is charged with expenses of completion of title by the trustees,
such as costs of valuations prepared for estate duty purposes, and
registration fees of confirmation. Brokerage and stamp-duties on
investments, and legal expenses regarding heritable properties sold
and purchased, are also chargeable to capital. Expenses of changes
in trustees, such as preparation and registration of deeds of
assumption and resignation, are also capital payments.

Solicitors' business accounts require to be analysed in detail.
Capital is chargeable with fees for ascertaining the amount of the
estate and debts due by deceased, negotiations re government
duties, realisation and re-investment of trust funds, protection of
the estate in legal processes, improvements to heritable property,
payment of legacies, and division of the residue.

Income is chargeable with fees re leases and factoring heritable property (except in respect of improvements), adjustments of income tax, and commission on collection of income.

It is usual to divide the fee for preparation and extension of trust accounts between capital and income according to the number of pages in each section. Engrossments in the sederunt book (or minute book) are generally charged to capital.

Audit fees are divisible between capital and income, generally according to the time required by each, and the auditor should state the appropriate figures.

V. *Death Duties :—*

Any estate duty, legacy duty, or succession duty, which may be payable out of trust funds, is chargeable to capital. Discount received on prepayment of such duty is income, and interest paid thereon is chargeable against income. (See pages 128, 134, 139 as to incidence of duties.

CHAPTER V

SUCCESSION

SUCCESSION to heritage is entirely distinct from succession to moveables Heritage and Moveables. although both are founded on common law. Heritage consists of land, houses, buildings, fixed machinery, and other fixtures in buildings, mines, minerals, timber, and rights secured upon land such as feuduties. Moveables include debts due to deceased, cash, sums in bank accounts, shares in companies, trademarks, and corporeal moveables, such as furniture and stock-in-trade. Unless executors are specifically excluded, heritable bonds are treated as moveable for purposes of succession. In calculating legal rights, however, they are always included in heritage. (31 and 32 Vic. c. 101, sec. 117.)

If, for example, an intestate dies survived by a wife and two sons, leaving no estate except heritable bonds for £3000 bearing 5% (£150 p.a.) the division is as follows :—

(1) *Legal rights :—*
  (a) *Widow.*—Terce is calculated as one-third of the income from the bonds, which for this purpose are heritage = £50 per annum.
  (b) *Children.*—There are no children's legal rights in heritage.
(2) *Intestate Succession.*—Subject to terce, the sons share the estate equally under the rules of intestate *moveable* succession. If the estate had been heritable the elder son would have taken the whole.

Conversion of property arises when heritage owned by deceased is Conversion of Property. subject to a completed contract of sale at the date of death, and in questions of succession such property is then treated as moveable. Similarly heritage includes for succession purposes the money required to meet the unpaid price of any heritable property purchased but not settled prior to death. A direction in the will to sell heritage converts it to moveable estate but power to sell has not this effect.

As regards illegitimate children's rights of succession, the subsequent Illegitimate Children. marriage of the parents renders the children legitimate if they were free to marry when the child was conceived. (See Kerr *v.* Martin, 1840, 2, D. 752.) On the death of an illegitimate child intestate (*i.e.* leaving no will) if the mother survives she has the same interest in the estate as she would have had if the child had been legitimate and she had been the only surviving parent. On the death intestate of the mother of an illegitimate child, leaving no surviving legitimate issue, such child and his issue are entitled to the same interest as they would have had if the child had been legitimate. (Legitimacy Act, 1926.)

If a deceased leaves a valid will he is said to have died testate. If Testate and Intestate. there is no will he is intestate, and partial intestacy may arise if the will does not completely dispose of the estate.

Legal Rights.

Under the common law, the estate of a deceased person remaining after payment of debts and government duties is subject to claims by the surviving spouse and family in respect of their legal rights which cannot be defeated by the terms of the will. The Married Women's Property Act, 1881, sec. 7, gave the right to claim legitim against the mother's estate in addition to the previously recognised claim against the father's estate. The balance after payment of legal rights is known

Dead's Part.

as dead's part and is divisible either in terms of the will or under the law of intestate succession as explained later (page 31).

Divorce.

Claims to husband's and wife's legal rights also arise on divorce except as regards *jus relicti* which only applies on death. (Harvey *v.* Farquhar, 1872, 10 M. (H.L.), 26, and Married Women's Property (Scotland) Act, 1881.) The innocent party is entitled to claim his or her rights as if the other had died. The guilty party has no rights, and if both are held guilty there are no claims available to either.

Ascertaining Legal Rights.

All legal rights vest in the successor on the date of death, and so the sums due are not conditional on any subsequent events. They are usually calculated on the valuation of the estate as at date of death, less expenses of realisation (Russel *v.* Attorney General, 1917, S.C. 28); but see Warrack *v.* Warrack's Trustees (1934, S.L.T. 302). Interest on the sums due is payable at the average rate earned by the trust funds (McCall, 1901, 3, F. 1065). Heritable bonds are deducted from the heritable property over which they are secured, in ascertaining the amount of the heritable estate. Various deductions are made from moveable property before the legal rights in respect of moveables are calculated, including deathbed and funeral expenses and estate duty on moveable property. (Russel *v.* Attorney General, 1917, S.C. 28.)

The beneficiaries must be informed of their legal rights and they then elect whether they will claim their legal rights or accept the provisions of the will and marriage contract. They cannot take both legal rights and provisions. The legal rights of the surviving spouse and children may be discharged in terms of an ante-nuptial marriage contract.

The legal rights are now detailed :—

Husband's Legal Rights.

I. *Husband's rights :—*

    (1) *Jus Relicti—*

Half of the wife's moveable estate vests in the surviving husband on her death if there are no surviving children. If there are surviving children the *jus relicti* is one-third of the moveable estate, unless they have all discharged legitim, when it is one-half.

    (2) *Courtesy—*

The surviving husband is vested in the liferent of the whole heritable estate owned by his wife, provided a child had been born of the marriage who was the mother's heir for however short a time.

Examples

    (1) Assume death of a woman owning heritable estate £1000 and moveable estate £1500, and survived by her husband and one child. The husband is entitled to one-third of the moveables as *jus relicti* = £500.

He may also claim the liferent of the whole heritage as courtesy.

The child's rights, as explained below, are one-third of the moveables as legitim = £500.

(2) In similar circumstances except that the child had discharged legitim, the husband is entitled to one-half of the moveables instead of one-third = £750.

The right to courtesy remains as before.

(3) If there was no child born of the marriage the husband would not be entitled to courtesy.

(4) If the wife had a surviving child by a former marriage this child would be the mother's heir, and any child of the second marriage would not be the mother's heir, so no claim to courtesy is then available.

II. *Wife's rights :—*

(1) *If intestate and no children survive, the first £500 of the estate.—*
In terms of the Intestate Husbands Estate Acts, 1911 and 1919, if the estate of a wholly intestate deceased husband is less than £500 the whole estate vests in the surviving wife, and if it is over £500 the first £500 vests in her, provided there is no lawful issue surviving. This must be met rateably out of heritable and moveable estate, that is, each contributes in proportion to the respective totals. The wife's other legal rights are calculated only after this has been met.

Wife's Legal Rights.

(2) *Jus relictae—*
Half of the husband's moveable estate vests in the surviving wife on his death if there are no surviving children. If there are surviving children the *jus relictae* is one-third of the moveable estate unless they have all discharged legitim, when it is one-half.

(3) *Terce—*
The surviving wife is vested in the liferent of one-third of the deceased husband's heritable estate, but the mansion house, superiorities, feuduties, and minerals are excluded. (Constables' Trustees *v.* Constable, 1904, 6, F. 826.) If terce is payable out of lands already subject to a prior terce, the second terce is known as lesser terce, calculated as one-third of the remaining two-thirds. On the death of the first liferentrix the second terce becomes a full terce.

Examples

(1) Assume the death intestate of a man survived by his wife and no children, and whose estate, wholly moveable, amounted to £1200.

The wife is entitled to the first £500 under the Intestate Husbands Estate Act, also *jus relictae* amounting to one-half of the remaining £700 = £350.

(2) Assume the estate had consisted of £1800 heritage and £600 moveables, but other facts as above.

The wife is entitled to the first £500 whereof £375 is chargeable against heritage and £125 against moveables— being taken in proportion from each fund. *Jus relictae* is then one-half of the remaining £475 moveables = £237, 10s. In addition she is entitled to terce, being the liferent of one-third of the remaining heritage. In practice, if the anticipated free annual income of the heritable property was £90 (after payment of the above sum of £375) the widow's share of £30 would be capitalised according to annuity tables. Assuming that at her age £400 would purchase a life annuity of £30 the executors would pay her £400 in full settlement of terce.

(3) Assume the death of a man owning estate of £1200, wholly moveable, and survived by his wife and one child.

The wife is entitled to *jus relictae* amounting to one-third of £1200 = £400. The child's rights are, as explained below, one-third of £1200 as legitim = £400.

(4) In similar circumstances, except that the child has either predeceased or discharged legitim, *jus relictae* is one-half of £1200 = £600.

Children's Legal Rights.

III. *Children's rights (not restricted to minors) :—*
   Legitim—
   Half of the deceased parent's moveable estate vests in the surviving children on the death of either father or mother if the other parent has predeceased. If the other parent survives the right is to one-third of the moveable estate unless *jus relictae* or *jus relicti* has been discharged by the survivor, when it is one-half. The children of children who have predeceased do not share in legitim, and the heir-in-heritage has no claim unless he collates (see below).

Examples

(1) Assume death of a man leaving a surviving wife and two children and whose moveable estate amounted to £1200. The wife is entitled to one-third = £400 as *jus relictae* and the children to one-third = £400 as legitim. This legitim fund is divisible equally between the children, each receiving £200.

(2) In similar circumstances except that the wife has either discharged her *jus relictae* or has predeceased, the legitim fund is one-half = £600 and each child receives £300.

(3) If there is also another child who has discharged legitim, the division is unaffected.

(4) If there had been another child who had predeceased leaving a family—grandchildren of deceased—they would have no legal rights, and the division is unaffected.

(5) If the estate was wholly heritable instead of moveable the children would have no legal rights.

COLLATION

Collation of Advances.

The collation of advances made by the father to his children is known as *Collatio inter Liberos*. (Collation of heritage by the heir is called *Collatio inter Haeredes* and this is dealt with under Intestate Succession, page 32.) A child claiming legitim must collate advances received from the parent in his lifetime unless the advances are exempt from collation. The following are the principal exemptions :—

(1) Advances from heritage.
(2) Cost of education.
(3) Alimentary payments and wages for services.
(4) Sums expressed to be in addition to legitim.
(5) Loans repayable to the executors and so forming part of the estate.

No difference arises in the division of the estate except as between the children, and the fund available for legitim plus advances to be collated is divisible equally among them.

In calculating the share of the child collating there is set off the sum advanced and only the net amount is payable to him.

Example

Assume advances had been made by deceased to his youngest son amounting to £300. The estate divisible amounted to £3900 (all moveable) and deceased was survived by his wife and three sons. If the youngest son wishes to claim legitim he must collate thus :—

	£	s	d
Legitim Fund one-third of £3900	£1300	0	0
Add Advances to be collated	300	0	0
Adjusted Legitim Fund	£1600	0	0
One-third whereof to each son	£533	6	8
Less Youngest son's advances	300	0	0
Net sum due to youngest son	£233	6	8

The total is divisible thus :—

	£	s	d
Wife—*jus relictae*—one-third of moveables (unaffected by collation)	£1300	0	0
Eldest son—one-third of adjusted legitim fund	533	6	8
Second son—one-third of adjusted legitim fund	533	6	8
Youngest son—one-third of adjusted legitim fund, less advances	233	6	8
	£2600	0	0
Dead's part, divisible in terms of Will	1300	0	0
	£3900	0	0

INTESTATE SUCCESSION

After the legal rights have been satisfied, the remainder of the estate Intestacy. is known as the dead's part, which may be divided in any way instructed by the testator in his will. If no valid distribution of any part of this has been made, such part falls into intestacy, that is either if no will has been made or the will does not dispose of the whole estate.

The estate is vested in the next of kin immediately on the death of the intestate. Moveable estate passes to the executors for distribution but heritage passes direct to the heir-in-heritage unless conveyed to the trustees in the trust disposition. If no relatives claim the estate the Crown inherits as *Ultimus Haeres*.

INTESTATE HERITABLE SUCCESSION

Rules of Intestate Heritable Succession.

This is extremely complicated and only an outline can be given here.

As a general rule heritage all passes without division to the nearest male heir, but if the nearest relatives are females all the females equally nearly related to deceased inherit in equal portions. They are known as *Heirs-Portioners*. (Further particulars as to their heirs' rights are given later, page 35.) There is no division even in such circumstances of certain classes of heritage (for example, where the heritage consists of a right of superiority) and these fall to the eldest heir-portioner. The lineal descendant of a deceased heir takes his place as heir, and this is known as *representation*. Succession descends to sons and daughters and their heirs in preference to passing to collaterals, *i.e.* brothers and sisters. The rule of *primogeniture* applies, and this means that the elder excludes the younger, except when the succession falls to collaterals, in which case it descends first to the younger members and their heirs in descending order, but if there are none it then ascends first to the next elder brother of deceased and his heirs, then to the next again, and so on.

Males are preferred to females of the same degree of relationship, and there is no succession by the mother or her representatives.

Collation.

If the heir-in-heritage claims legitim, or his share of dead's part in intestacy, he must collate the heritage, that is, throw it into the general estate for division along with the moveables among the same beneficiaries. This is called *Collatio inter Haeredes*. *Jus relicti* and *jus relictae* are not affected by collation.

Example

Assume the death intestate of a man who owned heritage £300 and moveables £6300, and leaving three sons surviving him. The eldest son is the heir-in-heritage who has no claim to legitim or dead's part unless he collates, so he is *prima facie* entitled only to heritage £300. The two others may then each claim one-half of the moveables as successors to both legitim and dead's part.

If the heir decides to collate the heritage, which is clearly to his advantage in this case, the whole estate is divisible equally among the three sons, and each receives £2200.

There is a further type of collation in terms of the Intestate Moveable Succession (Scotland) Act 1855, sec. 2, arising where an heir-in-heritage (being a descendant of the intestate or of his brothers and sisters) has predeceased the intestate. On the heritage passing to that heir's child he is entitled to collate the heritage, and, if he does not collate, his brothers and sisters and their descendants may do so. In the latter case the brothers and sisters are entitled to a share of the moveable estate, amounting to the excess over the value of the heritage which their predeceasing parent would have taken on collation if he had survived. (See Adam's Ex. *v.* Maxwell, 1921, S.C. 418 and Colville's J.F. *v.* Nicoll, 1914, S.C. 62.)

Examples

I. X died intestate, leaving heritage £60 and moveables £900 (total £960), having no children, but survived by two elder brothers S and T, and two nephews A and B both sons of a predeceasing younger brother Z. A being the elder son of a younger brother is the heir-in-heritage, and the moveables *prima facie* fall to S, T, and B equally = £300 to each. A, however, decides to collate so that the whole estate is then divisible according to the rules of intestate moveable succession —A and B each taking one-sixth = £160 (as representatives of Z) while S and T each take one-third = £320.

II. Assume the facts as above except that Z's family consisted of eight children instead of two. If A collates he receives only $\frac{1}{8} \times \frac{1}{3} \times 960 = £40$, so he does not collate but takes the heritage of £60. The brothers and sisters of A take advantage of their option to collate with the following effect :—

Assuming Z had survived he would have obtained one-third of the whole estate on collation = £320. The excess of this sum over the heritage is £260 and this is divisible among the seven brothers and sisters of A. The division is then made thus :—

A's seven brothers and sisters each £37, 2s. 10d.	£260
S—one-half of remaining moveables . .	320
T— do. do. . .	320
	£900
A—heritage	60
	£960

The following list gives the heirs in order of preference. The numbers correspond with the diagram appended, but those heirs who are not numbered are not shown on the diagram to avoid unnecessary complications :— *Priority of Heirs.*

Note.—Those marked * are heirs-portioners.

I. *Descendants :—*

1. Eldest *son.*
2. *Grandson* by eldest son.
    Then Eldest surviving *great-grandson* by him.
    Younger *grandson* by same son.
    Eldest surviving *great-grandson* by him, followed by younger grandsons and their representatives in the same way.
*3. Equally among *grand-daughters* by eldest son and their representatives (see No. 7 for explanation of representatives).
4. Younger *son.*
5. *Grandson* by younger son.
    Then his descendants as under 2.
*6. Equally among *grand-daughters* by younger son and their representatives (see No. 7).
*7.
*7A. }—*Daughters as heirs-portioners and their representatives :—*
*7B.

c

INTESTATE HERITABLE SUCCESSION

Order of priority

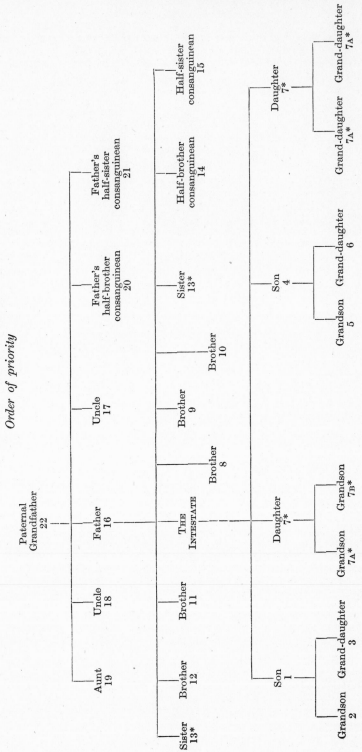

Notes (1) * = Heirs-portioners.
        (2) Representation applies throughout, *i.e.* the heirs of any of the above take their place if predeceased.

The division is made equally among surviving daughters and the descendants of any daughters who had predeceased, according to the following rules :—

(a) If a daughter has predeceased leaving as surviving issue one or more grandsons of the intestate, the eldest grandson is her representative and takes her share. If there are also grand-daughters they do not share.

(b) If a daughter has predeceased leaving as surviving issue one or more grand-daughters of the intestate and no grandsons, all the grand-daughters are her representatives (as heirs-portioners of an heir-portioner) and divide her share among them.

Note.—In the example on diagram there are two grandsons by the elder daughter (numbered 7A and 7B respectively). The elder grandson (7A) takes the share his mother would have received, and failing his survival the other grandson (7B) takes this share.

There are two grand-daughters by the younger daughter (both numbered (7A)) who divide equally the share their mother would have received.

II. *Collaterals :*—
8. Younger brother (then his heirs).
9.   do.   do.
10.   do.   do.
11. Elder brother   do.
12. Eldest brother   do.

Note.—The younger brothers are in order of seniority but the elder brothers are in the reverse order.

*13. Equally among sisters and their representatives.
14. Half-brother by same father (then his heirs, then other half-brothers).
*15. Equally among half-sisters by same father (and their representatives).

III. *Ascendants :*—
16. Father.
17. Father's younger brother (then his heirs).
18. Father's elder brother (then his heirs).
*19. Equally among father's sisters (and their representatives).
20. Father's half-brother by same father (then his heirs).
*21. Equally among father's half-sisters by same father (and their representatives).
22. Father's father (then his collaterals, etc., as for father above).

INTESTATE MOVEABLE SUCCESSION

Moveables pass on intestacy to those persons who are the nearest relatives of deceased, and the funds are divisible among them. In terms of the Intestate Moveable Succession (Scotland) Act, 1855, lineal descendants of a deceased relative take his place (by representation) if that relative was (1) a descendant, or (2) a brother or sister, or (3) a descendant of a brother or sister of the intestate. Such representation

Rules of Intestate Moveable Succession.

cannot be claimed by cousins if the estate is divisible among uncles and aunts of deceased, some of whom have predeceased the intestate leaving issue.

There is no rule of primogeniture or preference of males as in intestate heritable succession.   Maternal relatives have no claims.

Per Stirpes and Per Capita. Where children of predeceasing relatives are entitled by representation to share in the succession along with brothers and sisters of these persons, the basis of division is " *per stirpes* " (by stems, *i.e.* by family), that is, the share which would have been taken by the person predeceasing is divided among his children.   On the other hand, where the division is among persons of the same class, *i.e.* all grandchildren, the basis is " *per capita* " (by heads)—that is, equally among all participants.

Examples

(1) Assume the death of an intestate person with moveable estate of £2400 after settlement of legal rights, leaving two sons surviving and with one son who had predeceased leaving two children—grandchildren of the intestate.   The dead's part is primarily divided into three equal parts and one of these parts is subdivided into two equal parts for the grandchildren, thus :—

Surviving son A—one-third	. . . .		£800
do. B do.	. . . .		800
Family of C—(*Per Stirpes* basis) :			
Grandchild D—one-half of one-third		£400	
do. E do.		400	
		——	
			800
			——
			£2400
			═══

(2) Assume the death of an intestate person with moveable estate of £3600, all of whose sons had predeceased him, but who had four grandchildren surviving him, three being sons of A and one son of B.   C left no sons.   There are no claims for legitim, as no children survive.   The estate is divisible on the " *per capita* " basis, thus :—

Grandchild D (son of A) one-quarter	. .	£900
do. E do.	do.	. .	900
do. F do.	do.	. .	900
do. G (son of B)	do.	. .	900
			——
			£3600
			═══

Step-Brothers and -Sisters. Brothers and sisters by the same father but a different mother are known as half blood brothers and sisters consanguinean.   If they had the same mother but a different father they are half blood brothers and sisters uterine.   Half blood relatives are always postponed to those of full blood of the same line.

The following rules are provided by the Intestate Moveable Succession Acts, 1855 and 1919.

(1) If the intestate is survived by his father, and brothers and sisters of full blood or their descendants, but left no issue, the father is entitled to one-half.

Note.—If there are no surviving brothers and sisters nor descendants, the father is entitled to the whole estate by common law.

(2) Where an intestate leaves no issue and his father has predeceased him, the mother has the same rights as the father would have had.

(3) On the death of an intestate (without issue) whose father, mother, brothers and sisters consanguinean (and their descendants) have all predeceased him, the brothers and sisters uterine and their descendants are entitled to one-half of the estate.

The diagram on page 38 shows the basis of division of the dead's part *after payment of legal rights.*

The following explanations should be read with reference to the diagram :—

(1) *The order of priority* of classes is 1A, 1B, 1C, 2A, 2B, 2C, etc.
(2) *Division of Estate in ordinary circumstances :*
   (a) All surviving members of the same class take equal shares except where marked * (2A, 2B, 4A and 4B), described below.
   (b) If some members of an A class predeceased the intestate leaving issue, their shares fall to such issue (B class) and are divisible *per stirpes*—i.e., the children dividing equally the share their parents would have received.
   (c) If all members of an A class predeceased the intestate, the members of the B class divide the estate *per capita*, i.e. equally among all members of the class.
   (d) Similar rules apply between B and C classes, etc.
(3) *Special rules* re *father and mother* (2A and 2B) :
   (a) The father takes one-half share if any other members (except mother) of second class (2A, 2B, or 2C) survive the intestate and the other half falls to them. If the father but no others except mother survive, he takes the whole.
   (b) *The mother has the same rights as the father if he has predeceased,* but none otherwise.
   (c) Others of second class share the balance in the usual way.
(4) *Special rules* re *step-brothers and -sisters* (4A *and* 4B) :
   The uncles and aunts (4A) are entitled to one-half share divisible equally among them unless no brothers and sisters uterine or their descendants survive (4A and 4B), when they take the whole. The brothers and sisters uterine and their descendants share the balance in the usual way.
(5) *On death of a woman* the rights of her relatives and family are identical with those shown on diagram, which refers to a male intestate.
(6) No representation is admitted by descendants of deceased uncles and aunts. Thus a cousin gets nothing unless all the uncles and aunts are dead, when he shares equally with all others of the same class.

INTESTATE MOVEABLE SUCCESSION—(DEAD'S PART)

Order of priority on Death of a Male Intestate

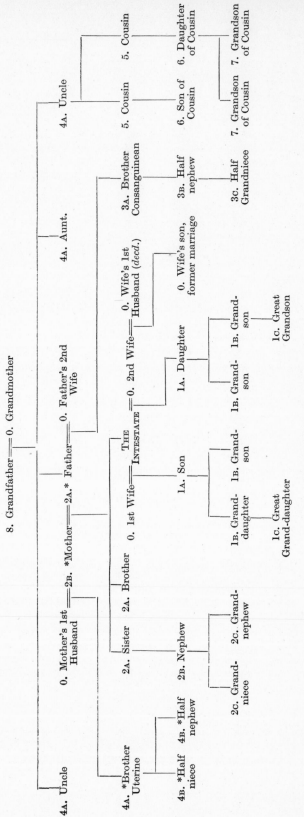

Notes.—Order of priority 1A, 1B, 1C, 2A, etc.
0 = No claim.

CHAPTER VI

INCOME TAX

On the death of any person his executors become liable to pay his income tax and sur-tax for the period to date of death (but excluding penalties), and similarly they may make any claims which he could have made had he survived. Assessments on heritable property under schedules A and B for the year of death should be apportioned between the deceased and his executors in proportion to the number of days applicable to each. Assessments on deceased under schedules D and E for the year of death must be adjusted to the actual income of the period prior to death, and the previous year's assessments may also require to be adjusted. Untaxed income receivable by the executors is assessable separately as a " new source " of income, without reference to sums received by the deceased. (F.A., 1926, secs. 29-31 ; F.A., 1927, secs. 23 and 45 ; and F.A., 1930, sec. 15.)

In connection with the adjustment of the income tax of the deceased the following points should be noted :—

(1) As regards dividends, etc., only sums *received* are included in his statutory income for period to date of death. (See Commissioners of Inland Revenue v. Henderson, 10, A.T.C. 292.)

(2) Personal allowances are available as follows :—

(a) *On death of a married woman* the husband includes her income to date of death in his statutory income and he is entitled to full married allowances for the fiscal year of death. He is not allowed a housekeeper allowance as a widower for the same year.

(b) *On death of a married man* the combined income of husband and wife up to that date is taken as his statutory income for the fiscal year of death, against which full married allowances are granted. The wife claims full allowances (not restricted by the short period) as a single person against her income from date of his death until the following 5th April.

(c) *On death of a single person* full allowances for fiscal year of death are granted against statutory income from the previous 5th April until death.

Executors and trustees must make returns of the income received by them, and they are liable to pay tax on all untaxed items. Sur-tax is a personal tax and trustees are not concerned with it except as regards incapacitated persons for whom they are guardians, or beneficiaries under discretionary trusts. (See F.A. 1933, sec. 34.)

As regards any beneficiary of a trust who is provided with a rent-free residence under the will, the net schedule A assessment of the house is regarded as his income and not the income of the trustees, but deductions are allowed against this for feuduty, ground-annual, minister's stipend, etc. (Lady Miller v. Commissioners of Inland Revenue, 1930, 15 T.C. 25).

Trustees cannot claim personal allowances but they are entitled to make claims for repayment or relief from tax payable, on the following grounds :—

(1) *Businesses—*

If trustees carry on a business either alone or in partnership, claims may arise for relief in respect of adjustments of tax on commencement or cessation of trading, or changes in partnership. Wear and tear allowances for plant are also given (I.T. Act, 1918, sch. D, cases I and II, rule 6 ; F.A., 1925, sec. 16 ; F.A., 1926, secs. 29-32 ; F.A., 1927, sec. 23 ; F.A., 1930, secs. 15-16). If a business is carried on by trustees, no earned income allowances are granted under present practice except (1) on the salaries paid to trustees or beneficiaries, or (2) on a share of profits earned by any beneficiary who is also a trustee and is actively engaged in the business (see Fry *v.* Shiels Trustees, 1915, 52, S.L.R. 103).

(2) *Trading Losses—*

Tax on losses in trade (including farming) may be recovered against other trust income, or the losses may be carried forward (I.T. Act, 1918, sec. 34, and F.A. 1926, sec. 33).

(3) *Farms—*

If farms are carried on by trustees, claims may be made for adjustment of assessments to actual profits, or alternatively they may be assessed under sch. D rules, which may be an advantage if there are losses, as these can then be carried forward (sch. B, rules 5 and 6).

(4) *Maintenance of Heritable Property—*

Where the average cost of repairs, insurance and management exceeds the statutory repairs allowance, a claim may be made under sch. A. V., rule 8, for relief on the excess up to the amount assessed under sch. A.

(5) *Empty Property—*

Tax may be recovered in respect of unoccupied houses under sch. A, VII, rule 4, and F.A. 1930, sec. 21.

(6) *Bank Interest—*

If interest is paid on bank overdrafts without deduction of tax a claim may be made for recovery of tax on this sum (I.T. Act, 1918, sec. 36).

(7) *Changes in Holdings of Investments—*

Where investments are held on which untaxed income is received, the assessments are normally on preceding year's basis but adjustments may be made when there are sales and purchases (F.A. 1922, sec. 17, and F.A. 1926, sec. 30).

(8) *Non-resident Beneficiaries—*

If the beneficiaries are resident abroad, the trustees should claim exemption from tax on their trust income from British government securities and foreign investments. (I.T. Act, sec. 46, and rules applicable to cases IV. and V.) If, for example, one half of the trust income belongs to a non-resident, claims will be admitted for repayment of tax paid on his half share of the trust income from securities which would be exempt if held in his own name.

(9) *Charities*—

Exemptions are conferred on charities (including religious, benevolent or educational societies) if they are of a permanent nature and bound by irrevocable deeds of trust. (See I.T. Act, 1918, sch. A. VI and sec. 37 ; F.A., 1921, sec. 30 ; and F.A., 1927, sec. 24.)

Charities may include in their claims certain income on legacies of residue due to them but not settled within one year after testator's death. (F.A., 1922, sec. 30.)

Difficulties frequently arise in connection with free of tax annuities. As a general rule an agreement to pay an annual sum free of tax is void, but this does not apply to annuities under wills (Pratt *v.* Gamble, 117, L.T. 545). If sur-tax is also to be paid by the trustees it should be specifically mentioned. *Free of Tax Annuities.*

Where there is a direction in the will to pay an annuity without deduction of tax, there may be a claim available to the trustees against the annuitant for recovery of the proportion of his personal income tax allowances applicable to the annuity. In the case of *re* Pettitt (38, T.L.R. 787) it was held that such a claim was competent, but the reverse was decided in the case of *re* Jones (1933, 47, T.L.R. 516) where the will directed the payment of such a sum as would, after the deduction of tax, provide a net sum of £X per annum. Further, in the case of Richmond's Trustees *v.* Richmond (1935, S.L.T. 336) it was decided by a majority of judges that the Pettitt basis was inapplicable. (The annuity in Richmond's case was directed to be paid free of income tax and super tax, and the annuitant had an independent income which was sufficient to cover all her reliefs.) Consequently it appears that the Pettitt decision is now considerably restricted in its application.

In ascertaining the trust's statutory income for any year, the tax recovered under the Pettitt basis for the previous year should be deducted from the payments made to the beneficiary. (See Public Trustee *v.* Day, Ch.D. 1922.) This method frequently produces variations in the figures from year to year, even if the annuity remains unchanged. Thus, assuming an annuity of £100 free of tax was payable to A, and the trustees received from him £20 in June 1933 in respect of their share of his allowances for 1932/3, the net outlay from trust funds in respect of the annuity for 1933/4 is taken as £80 equivalent to £106, 13s. 4d. gross less tax at 5s. = £26, 13s. 4d. This sum of £106, 13s. 4d. is entered by the annuitant as his income from the trust in his income tax return for that year.

If for any reason no sum is recovered from the annuitant the actual payments are grossed, thus when tax is at 5s. p. £1, £100 free of tax equals £133, 6s. 8d. less tax £33, 6s. 8d.

It is stated by the Inland Revenue that where there is no specific direction in the will as to the deduction of tax the trustees are deemed to possess the right of deduction, but if the right is not exercised the annuity is treated as tax compounded and not available for relief.

The calculation of sur-tax liability on tax-free annuities raises many complications, and the exact words of the will must be carefully noted. In the case of *re* Bowring (1918, 34, T.L.R. 575) it was held that the trustees' liability to super tax (now sur-tax) applicable to the annuity was to be calculated by taking the ratio of gross annuity to total income.

For example, assume there is a free of tax annuity which is equivalent to £3000 gross and the annuitant's personal income is £1000, the sur-tax for 1932/3 on £4000 is £171, 17s. 6d., whereof $\frac{3000}{4000}$ is payable by the trustees = £128, 18s. 1d., and the balance by the annuitant = £42, 19s. 5d.

Trusts' Statutory Income.

The statutory income of a trust must be ascertained annually because it is this sum which is allocated among the beneficiaries in the proportions directed in the will, for their personal income tax purposes. The actual payments to them may generally be ignored.

At present the Inland Revenue authorities prefer to adopt the year to 5th April for this purpose, but in certain circumstances where this is inconvenient and there are many investments it is permissible to adopt the date when the trust accounts close.

In ordinary circumstances the statutory income of a trust consists of (1) dividends receivable during the year, plus (2) the sums assessed under all schedules for the year in question, after deduction of relief in respect of business losses, cessation of trade, wear and tear, farm losses or profits less than schedule B assessment, maintenance of heritable property, unoccupied houses, bank interest paid, or sales of investments producing untaxed income (see page 40). Annual charges, e.g., feuduties, interest, annuities, etc., payable during the year, and management expenses, are deducted. Sums receivable or payable on account of bond-interest, feuduties, or ground-annuals, at Whitsunday term, are deemed to be applicable to the previous fiscal year.

Two cases have been decided as to expenses of management incurred under the testator's directions—Murray v. Commissioners of Inland Revenue (1926, 5, A.T.C. 607) and Macfarlane v. Commissioners of Inland Revenue (1929, 8, A.T.C. 227). The practical effect of these judgments is that only the net sum remaining after payment of the proportion of expenses chargeable to income (excluding factoring heritable property) is available for the beneficiaries, and under present practice the gross equivalent of the expenses is deducted. Thus expenses £9 are equivalent to £12 when tax is at 5s., and to £11, 5s. when tax is at 4s.

If the annual charges exceed the available income, as may occur, e.g., where annuities are partly payable out of capital, tax is payable to the Inland Revenue on the excess at the standard rate (I.T. Act, general rule 21).

An example of a trust income statement as required for Form R. 59 follows (rate of tax assumed to be 5s.) :—

A. (1) *Sources of Income*—

	Gross.	Tax.
Schedule A. assessment on Blackacre . .	£80	£20
do. D. do. on War Loan interest	20	5
£400 4% Funding Loan	16	4
	£116	£29
(2) *Charges*—		
Annuity to Miss J. Jones	16	4
	£100	£25

B. *Allocation of Income to Specific Purposes* .   . nil.

Note.—This refers, for example, to sums set aside for repayment
of bonds and not available for beneficiaries.

C. *Expenses Incurred by Trustees*—

Solicitors fees *re* Income . . .	£6 10 0
Audit fee—proportion	2 10 0
	£9 0 0

D. *Summary*—

Total amount of income less charges p. Section A   . £100

Less Income Tax on above do.	£25
Income allocated p. Section B . . .	*nil*
Expenses p. Section C	9
	— 34

Net Income £66

E. *Division of Income*—

	Fractional Share.	Share of Income.	Payments Made.
James Jones . . .	$\frac{1}{2}$	£33	£25
William Jones . . .	$\frac{1}{2}$	£33	£32

In the beneficiaries' claims the share of income of each is taken as
£44 less tax £11, irrespective of the actual payments. (The payments
to beneficiaries are taken into account if the trust is a discretionary trust,
but not otherwise, see page 44.) The effect of the above calculations
may be more easily understood thus :—

Income less charges	£100	£25
Less expenses—gross equivalent .	12	3
Income available for beneficiaries .	£88	£22

In liferented trusts where there are apportionments of income, there Apportion-ments.
are exceptions to the usual basis of ascertaining the statutory income
referred to above, thus :—

(a) *At Commencement of Liferent*—

As explained in a separate chapter (page 46) income which
accrued prior to the date of death of the testator is apportioned
to capital in the trust accounts. Under present practice such
sums are also excluded from the statutory trust income available
for beneficiaries for income tax purposes. These sums are not
income of any person, and are neither available for repayment
nor liable to sur-tax.

Where there is sur-tax liability on the liferenter's income
from the trust, the legal basis applicable to the first year's income
appears to be uncertain. One method, sometimes allowed
pending the ascertaining of the residue for legacy duty purposes,
is to take as his income the gross equivalent of payments made

to him out of trust income. Alternatively it is apparently allowable to take the statutory income of the trust in the usual way, but subject to deduction of sums apportioned to capital as explained in the preceding paragraph. Interest on estate duty is allowed as a deduction from income—the gross equivalent being taken because tax is not deducted from such interest. Interest of £18 is thus charged as £24 less tax £6. (As to income from residue see Marie Celeste *v.* Commissioners of Inland Revenue, 6 A.T.C. 17, and Commissioners of Inland Revenue *v.* Smith (C.A.), 15 T.C. 661.)

(b) *During the Liferent*—

Apportionments of dividends arising on sales and purchases of investments are ignored for income tax purposes because the Inland Revenue practice is based on English law which does not require such apportionments. On the death of an annuitant the amount of annuity accrued due since the last payment is not regarded as his income prior to death, and accordingly is excluded from the claim by his executor. This sum, however, must appear as a deduction from the trust income.

(c) *At Cessation of Liferent*—

Under present practice, the dividends accrued on the death of a liferenter are excluded entirely from statutory income and are not available for any repayment. There is an exception to this treatment where the liferenter's personal estate is bequeathed to residuary beneficiaries resident in the United Kingdom, as in such circumstances the "Residue Concession" described below is available to the latter individuals. On the cessation of a liferent owing to the marriage of the liferentrix the accrued income is similarly excluded entirely from her income, and from the trust income, although it might well be argued that this is inequitable.

Executry Residue Concession.

In any case where a taxpayer dies having bequeathed his estate to residuary beneficiaries resident in the United Kingdom, without liferent restrictions, the Inland Revenue permit a concessional treatment. In these circumstances all income received by executors either (a) on personal investments, or (b) accrued in respect of trust income liferented by the deceased, may be treated as divisible among these residuary legatees thus becoming available for repayment claims by them. The amount is restricted to such sums as legally form part of their shares of the residue and are actually received by them whether as income or capital.

In other cases not covered by this concession the income received by executors is not available for repayment claims by residuary legatees.

Discretionary or Contingent Trusts.

In trusts where payments to beneficiaries are at the trustees' discretion and the income is wholly or partly accumulated, the beneficiaries are said to have a contingent right to income. Such a right does not entitle them to treat the whole or fractions of the statutory income of the trust as their income, and instead only the gross equivalents of sums expended in each year may be taken. Claims for personal allowances may be made each year.

In trusts where accumulations of income are later payable to the beneficiary if he attains a specified age or marries, claims may be made

each year during the period of accumulation, on the basis referred to in
the preceding paragraph. In addition, on the vesting of the accumulations a claim may be made for any balance of personal allowances made
available by treating accumulated income as if it had originally belonged
absolutely to the beneficiary. This involves reopening each year's
income tax claims for the whole period of accumulation (I.T. Act 1918,
sec. 25, and F.A. 1923, sec. 30).

For income tax purposes, certain classes of *inter vivos* trusts are void, *Inter Vivos*
and the income from such trust funds is held to belong to the original *Trusts.*
owner of the funds (known as the " grantor "), thus possibly involving
him in sur-tax liability thereon.

The principal classes which are void are :—

(1) Trusts which without the consent of any other person can be
    revoked by the person granting the disposition of trust, so
    that the income can again be received by him.   (See Watson
    v. Wiggins (H.L.), 12 A.T.C. 161.)
(2) Trusts created for a period which cannot exceed six years.
(3) Trusts for the benefit of children, including step-children or
    illegitimate children of the grantor, if applicable to a period
    less than the lives of such children (except as shown below).

In general, trusts not falling under any of the above classes are
recognised as valid. There are also the following exceptions to the
above class (3) in which trusts are recognised :—

(*a*) If the funds will be held for the child absolutely at the close of
     the restricted period.
(*b*) If the only restriction on the period is the period of life of the
     grantor, *e.g.*, joint lives of the grantor and the child.
(*c*) If restrictions refer only to bankruptcy of the child.
(*d*) If the child has attained twenty-one years of age or has married,
     the trust is then recognised from the earlier of these two
     events.   (Finance Act, 1922, sec. 20.)

Incapacitated persons and children under twenty-one years of age *Parents' and*
are liable to income tax and sur-tax but entitled to the usual personal *Guardians'*
allowances. Their returns and claims must be signed by a parent or *Duties.*
guardian. Where an incapax has a vested right to income from a
trust, for tax purposes the proportion of statutory income of the trust
is taken in the usual way (see page 42). On the other hand if he is
entitled only to " discretionary " payments for education and maintenance, that is, allowances at the trustees' discretion, his income is
taken as the gross equivalent (at the standard rate of tax) of sums
expended, thus £90 expended = £120 gross less tax at 5s. = £30.

CHAPTER VII

APPORTIONMENTS

I. Introduction

APPORTIONMENT is the division of receipts and payments among those legally sharing them. The Apportionment Act 1870 states that rents, annuities, dividends, and other periodical payments in the nature of income shall, like interest on money lent, be considered as accruing from day to day, and shall be apportionable in respect of time accordingly.

This act is interpreted differently in England and Scotland, as in England, as a general rule, it is unnecessary to make apportionments on sales and purchases of investments, while in Scotland these are always made on transfers of income-bearing investments. In any case it is essential that the basis should be consistent throughout the period of the existence of the trust. Cases deciding questions of apportionment were Cameron's Factor 1873, 1 R. 21, and McLeod's Trust *v.* McLeod, 1916, S.C. 604.

When Required.

As a general rule apportionments are necessary when a trust is life-rented, and if annuities are payable which are declared to be restricted to the free income this constitutes a partial liferent and also involves apportionments. If specific instructions are given in the will all apportionments may be excluded.

Object.

Apportionments are required (1) at the beginning of a liferent, (2) on sales of property or investments during a liferent, (3) on purchases of property or investments during a liferent, and (4) at the end of a liferent. The object of apportionment is to find the true accrued income over the whole period of liferent ascertained primarily from the dividends, etc., received, but adjusting these by (1) excluding from income any sums receivable in respect of a period during which the investments were not held in liferent, and (2) conversely adding to income sums accrued but not received in that period.

Dividends.

The procedure in apportioning dividends may be summarised thus :—

I. All dividends received are *prima facie* income, but adjusted as shown in the next two paragraphs.

II. Deduct from income, and transfer to capital, apportionable sums, (1) at beginning of liferent, and (2) on purchases. At the beginning of a liferent these sums consist of the proportion of dividends which accrued prior to the date when the liferent commenced, *e.g.*, dividends declared after the testator's death but partly applicable to the period prior to his death. On purchases, the apportioned sums are made up of the proportion of dividends received after purchase but which accrued prior to the date of purchase.

III. Add to income, and deduct from capital, apportionable sums (1) on sales, and (2) at end of liferent. On sales the apportioned sums are made up of the proportion of the sale proceeds which represents accrued dividend on the investments. At the end of the liferent the accrued dividends are similarly calculated on all investments.

Rents are usually allocated between purchaser and seller in terms of the agreement between them, and the proportion of rates, taxes, and other accrued burdens is usually deducted from these rents. The sale price of a heritable property is thus entirely exclusive of accrued income while the price of an investment generally includes the accrued dividend. Rents receivable, and feuduties and rates and taxes, etc., payable are apportioned at the beginning and end of the liferent according to the same principles as dividends, as explained later (page 55). Heritable
Properties.

In preparing trust accounts the apportionments should always be fully detailed. The examples in this book show these by cross-entries transferred from income account to capital account and *vice versa*, but, alternatively, entries may be shown in a columnar statement analysing capital and income. In the following pages, questions arising in apportionment are discussed, first as to dividends and income tax thereon, and second as to rents and burdens on property. Form of
Accounts.

II. APPORTIONMENTS OF DIVIDENDS AND INCOME TAX THEREON

Other things being equal, the value of stocks and shares is assumed to increase *daily* by the amount of accrued dividend or interest, and when a dividend is received the value is assumed to decrease by the net amount thereof. In practice, many other factors affect the market value from day to day.

As an example, assume 5% tax free debentures are issued at 96%. One day after the issue the amount of accrued interest is £0·0137 on each £100—or approximately 3d.—being $\frac{1}{365}$ of £5, and the next day 6d., then 9d., and so on. (Apportionments are usually taken to the nearest penny.) Assume that after six months expire, the debentures have a market value of 95% " cum. div.," which means that the half-year's interest is included in the price. If the debentures are sold at this date and price, the accrued interest is credited to income leaving a net capital value of $95 - 2\frac{1}{2} = 92\frac{1}{2}\%$.

If the interest is not payable until 14 days after the expiry of the six months to which it refers, the accrued interest on a sale on the 12th day of this period is (1) first half-year's interest £2, 10s., (2) interest for 12 days of second half-year $= \frac{12}{365}$ of £5 = 3s. 3d., thus making the total sum accrued, £2, 13s. 3d.

A summary of Stock Exchange procedure as to dividends may be of interest. A contract note is issued on the date of each transaction which must be stated as either (1) for cash settlement, or (2) for settlement on a specified date—known as settlement day. Any dividends declared after the date of the transaction belong to the buyer. After the declaration of a dividend, transactions may be either " cum. div." or " ex. div."—the former meaning that the buyer is entitled to the dividend and the latter meaning that the buyer is not entitled to it (the seller taking it instead). Apart from certain British government Sales and
Purchases.

securities which are marked ex. div. some weeks before due date of interest payment, the ex. div. marking generally commences at or about the actual dividend or interest date.

Sometimes owing to the closing of transfer books a dividend is paid to a seller of shares cum. div., in which case he is liable to pay it over to the buyer. The latter should, of course, see that all due dividends on purchases are actually received.

Before apportionments are made, dividends which are received and paid away must be excluded from the cash transactions. For an example of apportionments on a sale cum. div., see No. 10 apportionment in specimen account (page 103).

The date to be taken as the date of the sale or purchase is the date of the contract if the transaction is " for cash," and the specified " date for settlement " in other cases. (See Londesborough v. Somerville, 1854, 19 Beav. 295.)

Ascertainment of Income. The general rule is that dividends accrue during the period in respect of which they are declared or expressed to be payable. The first day of a period is excluded in apportionment calculations—e.g., 1st to 11th January is ten days. The practical application of this rule depends on information contained in the dividend warrants and reports issued by the companies, which are sometimes lacking in detail and consistency. The report should be taken in preference to the warrant if there is doubt.

Half-Yearly Dividends. Dividends and interest may be declared in respect of each quarter-year or half-year, as is done in the case of British government securities. Rents and feuduties are also payable half-yearly. The apportionment of such sums presents some difficulty, and three methods are available— each producing slightly different results. The method adopted at the beginning should be continued throughout the trust's life, as variations in method might have the effect of benefiting some beneficiaries at the expense of others, while consistency of method produces a more equitable result.

First Method—

In apportioning a dividend under this method the calculation is based on the number of days in the quarter or half-year for which it is declared. Thus if a dividend of £13, 11s. 3d. is payable in respect of the half-year to 1st June 1933 the sum accrued from 1st December 1932 to 2nd February 1933 is :—

$$\frac{63}{182} \times £13, 11s. 3d. = £4, 13s. 11d.$$

Note.— 63 days from 1st December 1932 to 2nd February 1933.
182 days from 1st December 1932 to 1st June 1933.

This method is largely adopted for examination purposes, but is not free from criticism. It is rather complicated in operation, as the calculations cannot be done by using interest tables, which may conveniently be used for the other two methods.

Second Method—

Under this method the first half-year's dividend received by the trustees is treated as an interim dividend, and the second half-year's dividend as a final dividend, both on account of the first year of the company during which the investment was held. The third dividend is treated as an interim dividend for the second year and so on.

Thus to find the accrued dividend up to the date of sale of the investment referred to in the above example (2nd February 1933) the amount depends on the date of purchase.

(a) If the December payments are to be treated as interim dividends the amount is :—

Accrued dividend from 1st June 1932 to 2nd Feb. 1933

(246 days)$=\dfrac{246}{365}\times$£27, 2s. 6d.   .   .   £18   5   8

Less interim distribution received 1st Dec. 1932 .   13 11   3

£4 14   5

(b) If on the other hand the June payments are to be treated as interim dividends the amount is :—

Accrued dividend from 1st Dec. 1932 to 2nd Feb. 1933

(63 days)$=\dfrac{63}{365}\times$£27, 2s. 6d. £4 13   8

This method is recommended by Professor Annan on the grounds that the original contract for payment of interest, dividend, or rent, specifies the *annual* payment to be made, and that if the warrants issued with dividends, etc., are not consistent with this contract, they should be ignored. The number of days in a " half-year " may be 180, 181, 182, 183, 184, 185, or 186, but the first method allocates each half-yearly payment to one of these unequal periods, resulting in variations in the daily yield.

Under the second method, however, the interest is treated as accruing equally in respect of each day of the year, which is a more logical result. Where it is impossible to apply this method, owing to difficulty in ascertaining which half-yearly payment is the interim and which is the final distribution, Professor Annan recommends that the third method should be used.

Third Method—

Under this method the accrued dividend is taken at the *annual rate* for the number of days since the close of the period up to which the previous dividend was paid.

Thus in the circumstances given in the second example the accrued dividend is calculated as shown there under (b) = £4, 13s. 8d.

This method produces approximately correct results in a simple manner, and is frequently adopted in practice.

Where the period of apportionment includes 29th February in a Leap-Years. leap-year it is necessary, in theory, to include this day. The effect on annual apportionments is to make these on a basis of 366 days instead of 365, giving the answer in multiples of 1/366. In practice, as the difference is small, 29th February may generally be ignored.

Special difficulties arise in connection with certain government Government issues which are quoted " ex. div." before the date of payment, although Securities. interest is paid on the basis of the half-year to date of payment. This means that purchasers during the period between ex. div. date and date of payment receive no interest for this period, and conversely sellers receive interest on stock sold possibly some weeks previously. In theory, the price is assumed to discount this interest. For example, the correct basis of apportionment is to take the interest on $3\frac{1}{2}\%$ War Loan as accruing from 1st June and 1st December. There are 183 days from 1st June to 1st December and 182 days from 1st December to 1st June, so if the half-yearly method is adopted (First method, page 48), apportionments should be taken as multiples of 1/183 or 1/182, respectively, but see page 49 as to annual basis. When sales and purchases take place between the date when the stock is marked " ex. div." and the date of payment of interest the treatment is as follows :—

On Sales—

The accrued interest for period from date of sale until date of payment of interest is applicable to capital, and must be subtracted from income and added to the sale price. Thus, if £2000 4% Funding Loan is sold ex. div. on 5th April 1933 the interest for half-year to 1st May 1933 is afterwards received although the stock is no longer owned. The apportionment is :—

(a) *Income Account*—

1st May 1933. Received half-year's interest to date £40 less tax at 5s. £10	£30	0 0
Less Applicable to capital from 5th April 1933 (date of sale) to date (26 days) £5, 13s. 11d. less tax £1, 8s. 6d. .	4	5 5
Balance applicable to income	£25	14 7

(b) *Capital Account*—

5th April 1933. Proceeds of sale of stock as per contract note, less expenses	£2190	0 0
Add Accrued interest due by income . .	4	5 5
	£2194	5 5

On Purchases—

The accrued interest from date of purchase until date of payment of interest is applicable to income and must be added to the purchase price. Thus, if £1000 4% Funding Loan is bought ex. div. on 15th October 1934, no interest is receivable until 1st May 1935 for the half-year from 1st November 1934. The apportionment is :—

1st Nov. 1934. Amount of accrued interest from 15th October 1934 to date (17 days) applicable to income £1, 17s. 3d., less tax at 4s. 6d., 8s. 5d.	£1	8 10

The sum of £1, 8s. 10d. is added to the purchase price thus :—

Price as per contract note, including expenses .	£1120	0 0
Add Accrued interest due to income . .	1	8 10
Adjusted capital cost of investment . .	£1121	8 10

As explained in the chapter on " The Preparation of Trust Accounts " Foreign
Exchange.
(page 64), foreign cash transactions are converted to sterling, either
(1) at the rate actually realised (if remitted at once), or (2) at the rate
ruling at the time (if balances are retained abroad). All these sterling
sums are apportioned in the usual way, but special difficulties may
arise as to anticipated dividends. (See page 53.)

In terms of the Apportionment Act, 1870, apportionments must take Income Tax.
into account all " just allowances " from income. This clearly covers
income tax deducted from dividends at the source. The question of
apportionment of income tax payable on assessments is not definitely
settled by statute, but in equity such tax ought to be apportioned in the
same way as the income on which it is charged. In practice, therefore,
net dividends from which tax has been deducted before receipt should
be apportioned on the amounts actually received. Where dividends
or interests are received gross, tax should be deducted for the purpose
of apportionment, or a separate apportionment of the tax may be made
instead when the assessment is paid. It is necessary to keep in view
also that separate assessments are made on the executors in respect of
(a) income received prior to date of death of deceased, all of which tax
is a debt due by deceased, and (b) income received after death, tax on
which is dealt with as noted above.

On the Stock Exchange, bonds such as United Kingdom Treasury
Bonds are dealt in at a price exclusive of interest. For example, if a
5% Bond is quoted on 1st August at 101% and at the same price on
2nd August—the previous half-year's interest having been paid on
1st June—a purchaser on 1st August pays 101%, plus 16s. 9d.% for
accrued interest and on 2nd August 17s.%—the difference of 3d.%
being one day's interest. Tax is not deducted from this interest which
is part of the price and not taxable.

Assume £1000 of the above 5% Bonds were purchased

on 1st August 1932 at 101%	.	.	.	£1010	0 0
Plus interest from 1st June (61 days) .		.	.	8	7 2
		Actual sum payable .	.	£1018	7 2

In the trust accounts when the first interest is received on 1st December
1932, £25 less tax £6, 5s. = £18, 15s., the following apportionment is
necessary :—

Proportion of interest applicable to capital, from
1st June to 1st August 1932 (61 days) £8, 7s. 2d.

less tax £2, 1s. 9d.	.	. . . .		£6	5 5

The capital cost as adjusted in the accounts is :—

Price of bonds plus interest (excluding tax)	.	.	£1018	7 2
Less interest applicable to capital (less tax)		.	6	5 5
			£1012	1 9

(The effect is to add tax on the accrued interest to the net
capital value.)

Where liferenters are abroad and not liable to United Kingdom tax, all apportionments of income must be made exclusive of tax on income from War Loan, Funding Loan, Victory Bonds, and foreign investments, which are exempt in such circumstances.

Before the balance of income is paid over to the executors of a deceased liferenter, provision must be made for all income tax assessments outstanding, thus assuring that all apportionments of income due to the liferenter are made less tax.

III. General Notes on Apportionments of Dividends

1. *At Commencement of Liferent*—

After taking as *prima facie* income all dividends received, the proportion of each dividend applicable to the period before commencement of the liferent is deducted and treated as a capital receipt. These sums are best treated in the accounts as partial realisations of the investments.

(In the examples below, it is assumed that the liferent commences at the date of the testator's death, but a liferent may commence on the setting aside of a fund in terms of a scheme of division. In such cases the procedure is similar, and the rules of apportionment apply as if the words " date of division " were substituted for " date of testator's death.")

For example, if a dividend is received for year to 1st December 1933 amounting to £365 net, and deceased died on 28th April 1933, the amount applicable to capital for period from 1st December 1932 to date of death (148 days) is $\frac{148}{365} \times £365 = £148$. Several points require special mention here :—

(a) *Interim and Final Dividends*—

(i) *Where an interim dividend was received by the testator and a final dividend by the trust.*

If the period for which the dividend is declared ended before date of death, the whole final dividend is capital. If not, on receipt of the final dividend add this dividend to the interim dividend to give the total dividends for the period, and take as income the proportion of this total from the date of testator's death until the close of the period for which the dividends were declared. The remainder of the final dividend after deduction of this sum is applicable to capital. See paragraph (b) as to cases where the final dividend is insufficient to meet the sum due to income.

(ii) *Where no interim dividend was received by the testator on account of the year current at date of his death*—

Each dividend received by the trust must be apportioned between capital and income on the basis of the number of days of the period to which it applies which are before and after the testator's death respectively. Some dividends may be entirely applicable to capital.

(b) *Dividends which are " in bonis " of the Deceased*—

If an interim dividend received prior to date of death was greater than the final dividend received by the trustees, on apportionment as in paragraph (a) (i) there may be a sum due from capital to income to make up the final dividend to the total amount due to income. The procedure here is—make no apportionments and take the whole final dividend as income. This is based on the common law rule which prevents trustees from treating as income any sums which are " in bonis " of the testator, and the Apportionment Act by implication excludes sums received by deceased. All dividends due and exigible before date of death are " in bonis."

(c) When investments are sold during the period of the first account of the trust, it is preferable for simplicity in the accounts to make only one apportionment covering the two distinct calculations arising (1) at beginning of liferent, and (2) on sale. For this purpose, dividends received on investments sold are added to the price realised on sale of each, and one calculation is then made of the sum due to income account according to the number of days in the period from the commencement of the trust until the date of sale of the investment. The rate of dividend may require to be anticipated as explained below.

The above rule cannot be usefully applied in the following cases which require two distinct apportionments—one at the commencement of the trust and one on sale of the investment.

(i) Investments on which quarterly or half-yearly dividends are declared, on which at least one dividend is received prior to sale.

(ii) Investments on which annual dividends are declared, on which the final dividend for any year is received prior to sale.

2. *Apportionments on Sales—*

The price of investments sold is assumed to include the accrued dividend from the date up to which dividends have been received prior to the sale. In order to estimate this, where investments are not fixed-interest-bearing, it is necessary to anticipate the rate of dividend for the year of sale, as explained below, taking into account *only the facts known at date of sale.* The amount of accrued dividend is subtracted from the capital proceeds of sale and credited to income account. See below as to calculations where an interim dividend has been received.

Apportionments (1) on sales, and (2) at close of liferent, must be made on the basis of dividends anticipated at the time and not in the light of subsequent information. (In other apportionments, under present practice, the subsequent facts are usually taken into account, as this can be done without difficulty.) Income tax rates must be anticipated similarly, and also the rate of exchange where dividends are receivable in foreign currencies. Questions as to anticipated rates may require negotiation with the liferenter or his executors if large sums are involved. In calculating the rate of anticipated dividends, the following basis may conveniently be adopted unless reliable contrary information is available at the time of sale regarding the probable rate :— *[margin: Anticipated Rates.]*

(1) If no interim dividend is yet declared for the current year take the previous annual rate for the year.

(2) If an interim dividend has been declared and it is the same as the previous year's, take the previous annual rate for the year.

(3) If an interim dividend has been declared and it is different from the previous year's rate, apply the same ratio to the year's rate. Thus, if the interim dividend is 1% against 2% the final dividend should also be taken as one-half of the previous year's rate.

The total accrued dividend is calculated since the end of the period for which the last final dividend has been paid; this sum is taken as income, less any interim dividends already received.

3. *Apportionments on Purchases*—

The price of each investment is assumed to include the accrued dividend since the date up to which the last dividend has been paid. The first dividend received after purchase is apportioned so that the sum accrued prior to the date of purchase is taken as applicable to capital, and deducted from the cost price. It is sometimes argued that in equity the basis of anticipating dividends is also applicable here, but see sec. 3 of Apportionment Act as to recovery of sums when payable.

For convenience, interim and final dividends may be added together and apportioned in one sum if both appear in the same trust account.

If the trust account closes between the date of purchase of an investment and the receipt of the first dividend, the apportionment of the first dividend should be shown in the account in which it appears. This is preferable to making a pro forma apportionment in the account which shows the purchase, as difficulty may arise if the rate of dividend changes.

4. *Apportionments on Cessation of Liferent*—

All dividends accrued at this date, since the date to which the last final dividend is paid, must be anticipated according to information available at the time, in the same way as apportionments on sales (see above). The total is treated as income due to the liferenter's executors. The corresponding entry in capital account may be made in two ways :—

(1) The value of the investments at the close of the account may be increased by the addition to each investment of the dividend accrued thereon. This is the converse of the usual procedure at the beginning of the liferent, when the accrued dividends should have been subtracted from the value of investments as at date of death, and treated as partial realisations of investments.

(2) The total accrued dividends may be shown as a single capital payment. This method is generally adopted in practice, but the first is more correct in theory.

It is uncertain whether the same rules, regarding dividends which are " in bonis " of the deceased liferenter, apply as they would do at the testator's death (see page 52). In equity it appears logical to use the same basis, but no case appears to have been decided on the point. If the interim dividend received during the lifetime of the liferenter is greater than the anticipated income accrued for the period, it is, therefore, usual to make no apportionment, and the final dividend received after his death is all taken as applicable to capital.

IV. Apportionments of Rents and Burdens on
Heritable Property

The principles are as described above in connection with dividends,
but there are certain difficulties which are now described. House rents
are generally payable half-yearly on 15th May (Whitsunday) and 11th
November (Martinmas) but the removal terms are 28th May and 28th
November. The former dates must be taken for apportionments
(Campbell, 1849, 11 D. 1426, and Horsburgh, 1892—unreported).
Grazing rents and shooting rents are apportioned over the actual period
of occupation and not over the whole year (Earl of Glasgow's Trustees v.
Clark, 1889, 16 R. 545).

Farms may be either arable or pastoral, and different methods are Farm Rents.
applicable to each. If they are arable farms the legal term of entry
is Martinmas and the first half-year's rent is normally payable at the
following Whitsunday. In pastoral farms, on the other hand, the legal
term of entry is Whitsunday and the first half-year's rent is payable
on entry—the last half-year's rent of the previous tenant having been
due at the previous Martinmas. The above basis is the " legal term "
basis, but by agreement rents may be payable at other terms—known
as " conventional terms." These may be either forehand (in advance)
or backhand (in arrear), generally either six months or one year.
Forehand farm rents seldom arise in present practice, and accordingly
it seems unnecessary to discuss these further.

Apportionments of pastoral farm rents cause most difficulty because
it is uncertain to which period these legally apply. (See Baillie v.
Fletcher, 1915, 1 S.L.T. 364.)   Such rents should be treated as applicable
to the crop-year ending at Martinmas.   The half-year's rent legally due
on entry at Whitsunday is thus taken as accruing during the preceding
half-year when the crop was growing, despite the fact that the tenant
had then no right of possession.   (The rent may be payable backhand,
but it still applies to that period.)

Arable farm rents due at the legal terms are apportioned in respect
of the period up to the due date of payment, and require no further
comment.   Backhand arable rents are apportioned over the period to
which they apply as stated in the lease.   For example, the first payment
of rent due six months backhand is payable one year after entry, but
is apportioned over the first half-year of occupation.

The following are the burdens on heritable property and the periods Burdens.
applicable to each :—

1. *Feuduties and Ground Annuals* are payable at Whitsunday
   and/or Martinmas either yearly or half-yearly at the end of
   the period, under deduction of tax.

2. *Local Rates.*—These are payable to County Councils and Burgh
   Councils usually in respect of the year to 15th May, at dates
   varying according to local custom. Rates in Scotland are
   separately charged on owners and occupiers and are assessed
   on the annual rental value. (In Edinburgh the year of
   assessment ends on 28th May.)

   In terms of the Local Government Scotland Act, 1929,
   the assessable value for rating of (a) agricultural lands and
   heritages is the annual value less a deduction of $87\frac{1}{2}\%$, and

of (b) industrial and freight transport lands and heritages similarly less a deduction of 75%. These reductions are known as " De-rating." Further, occupiers of agricultural lands under leases dated prior to 1st June 1928 are entitled to recover from the owners a sum equal to $2\frac{1}{2}$ times the owners' rates for each year. Occupiers of industrial lands and heritages under such leases are entitled to recover three times the owners' rates for each year.

3. *Land Tax* is payable to the Inland Revenue in respect of the year to 24th March, and the tax is due on the preceding 1st January.

4. *Income Tax Schedule A* is payable in respect of ownership of heritable property for the year to 5th April, and the tax is due on the preceding 1st January. The assessment may be made on the tenant and in that case the tax is recoverable from the owner by deduction from the next payment of rent.

5. *Income Tax Schedule B* is payable in respect of occupation of land and is usually due in two instalments on 1st January and 1st July in respect of the year to the 5th April falling between the dates of payment.

6. *Ministers' Stipends* are payable to local ministers or to the Church of Scotland General Trustees by the owner of heritable property. These may accrue either (a) for the crop-year which is generally taken as the year to Martinmas, or (b) half-yearly at Whitsunday and Martinmas, and payment is made under deduction of tax.

7. *Teinds* are payable to the titulars, *i.e.*, the present owners of the title. They are payable either for the crop-year (see stipends) or half-yearly at Whitsunday and Martinmas, and income tax is deducted.

8. *Insurance Premiums* are payable in advance, from the date the insurance is effected. The owner usually pays for insurance of buildings and the tenant for insurance of contents or stocks on farms, but this is subject to agreement and other arrangements may be made.

Term Days.   The term days in Scotland are as follows :—

		Removal term	
Candlemas	Rent due 2nd February.	Removal term	28th February.
Whitsunday	do. 15th May.	do.	28th May.
Lammas	do. 1st August.	do.	28th August.
Martinmas	do. 11th November.	do.	28th November.

For insurance purposes, the following English term days should be noted :—

Lady Day—25th March.   Michaelmas—29th September.
Midsummer—24th June.   Christmas—25th December.

CHAPTER VIII

EXAMPLES OF APPORTIONMENTS

I. Examples of Apportionments of Dividends

I. *At Commencement of Liferent—*
Assume the death on 12th June 1933 of X whose estate is liferented
by his widow. His investments consisted of £1000 4% deb. stock A.B.
Co. and 2000 £1 ord. shares A.B. Co.

(1) *Apportionment of Interest on £1000 4% Deb. Stock A.B. Co.—*
On 1st August 1933 interest is received for the half-year to
1st June 1933, and this is all applicable to capital, as it
refers to a period before date of death. On 1st February
1934 the half-year's interest to 1st December 1933 is received
=£20 less tax £5 = £15, apportioned as follows :—

Sum applicable to capital—from 1st June (date to which last interest accrued) to 12th June 1933 (date of death)—11 days = £1, 4s. 1d. less tax 6s.	.	.	.	.	.	£0 18 1
Balance applicable to income	.	.	.	.		14 1 11
						£15 0 0

(2) *Apportionment of Dividend on 2000 £1 Ord. Shares A.B. Co.—*
On 30th September 1933, a 4% dividend is received for year to
1st August 1933 = £80 less tax £20 = £60, apportioned as
follows :—

Sum applicable to capital—from 1st August 1932 (date to which last dividend accrued) to 12th June 1933 (date of death)—315 days $=\dfrac{315}{365}$ ×£60	.	.	.	.	.	£51 15 7
Balance applicable to income	.	.	.	.		8 4 5
						£60 0 0

II. *On Sales and Purchases—*
(1) Assume that the above holding of £1000 4% deb. stock A.B. Co.
is sold on 1st March 1934. The proportion of the sale price
applicable to income represents interest from 1st December
1933 (to which last interest accrued) to 1st March 1934 (date
of sale)—90 days=£9, 17s. 3d. less tax £2, 9s. 4d. = £7, 7s. 11d.
(2) Assume that the proceeds of this sale are re-invested on 20th
March 1934 in £1000 4½% deb. stock C.D. Co. on which the
next interest is due on 1st April 1934 for half-year to that
date. When this interest is received = £22, 10s. less tax
£5, 12s. 6d. = £16, 17s. 6d., it is apportioned as follows :—

57

Sum applicable to capital from 1st October 1933
(date to which last interest accrued) to 20th
March 1934 (date of purchase)—170 days
= £20, 19s. 2d. less tax £5, 4s. 10d.   .   .   £15 14   4
Balance applicable to income   1   3   2

                             £16 17   6

III. *At Cessation of Liferent*—

Assume the death of the liferenter of the above trust on 3rd April
1934. The accrued sums apportioned to income as at that date are as
follows :—

(1) *On* 2000 £1 *Ord. Shares A.B. Co.*—

Sum accrued at 4% less tax at 5s. p. £1 (being the
anticipated rate) from 1st August 1933 (date to
which last dividend accrued) to 3rd April 1934
(close of liferent)—245 days $= \dfrac{245}{365} \times £60$.   .   £40   5   6

Note : Dividend p.a. = £80 less tax £20 = £60.

(2) *On* £1000 4½% *Deb. Stock C.D. Co.*—

Sum accrued from 1st April (date to which last
interest accrued) to 3rd April 1934 (close of
liferent) = 2 days = 4s. 11d. less tax 1s. 3d.   .   0   3   8

Note : The interest is taxable at the anticipated rate
of 5s. p. £1.

Total accrued income as at 3rd April 1934   .   .   £40   9   2

II. EXAMPLES OF APPORTIONMENTS OF RENTS, ETC.

I. *At Commencement of Liferent*—

Assume the death on 11th August 1930 of a testator owning two
farms—Blackacre—a pastoral farm with rent payable at legal terms—
and Whiteacre—an arable farm with rent payable six months backhand.
The following apportionments are required :—

(1) *Rents Receivable*—

(a) *Blackacre.*—The first half-year's rent of a pastoral farm
due at legal terms is payable on entry. The present tenant
occupied the farm as from Whitsunday 1930 and paid one
half-year's rent, £182, 10s. at that term. The next payment
of rent (at Martinmas 1930) is legally held to refer to the
half-year immediately preceding the due date of payment,
i.e., the half-year to Martinmas 1930, and is apportioned as
follows :—

Proportion applicable to capital—from 15th May
to 11th August 1930 (88 days) $= \dfrac{88}{365}$ of rent
for year to 15th May 1931 of £365   .   .   £88   0   0
Balance applicable to income   .   .   .   94 10   0

                             £182 10   0

(b) *Whiteacre.*—The first half-year's rent of an arable farm due six months backhand is payable one year after entry. The present tenant occupied the farm as from Martinmas 1929 and had therefore paid no rent prior to death of the testator. The rent received at Martinmas 1930 in terms of the lease refers to the first half of year to that date and was legally due at Whitsunday 1930, apart from the six months' backhand arrangement. Rents due before date of death, whether actually received or not, are not apportioned, but fall wholly to capital as " in bonis " of the deceased under common law. This rent accordingly is applicable to capital. The rent received at Whitsunday 1931 is apportioned as follows :—

Sum applicable to capital from 11th November
   1929 to 11th August 1930 (273 days) =
   $\frac{273}{365} \times$£182, 10s. £136 10 0
   Less half-year's rent received on 11th November
   1930 . . . . 91 5 0

                            £45 5 0
Balance applicable to income 46 0 0

                            £91 5 0

(2) *Burdens Payable*—
  (a) *Feuduty* of £10 payable under deduction of tax annually at Martinmas :—
    On 11th November 1930 the following apportionment is made :—
    Proportion applicable to capital—from 11th
    November 1929 to 11th August 1930 (273
    days)=$\frac{273}{365} \times$£7, 15s. (being £10 less tax £2, 5s.) £5 15 11
    Balance applicable to income . . . 1 19 1

                            £7 15 0

  (b) *Local Rates.*—On 1st January 1931 £40 is payable in respect of owner's rates for year to 15th May 1931. The proportion applicable to capital is from 15th May to 11th August 1930
    (88 days)=$\frac{88}{365} \times$£40 . . . . . £9 12 10
    Balance applicable to income 30 7 2

                            £40 0 0

  (c) *Income Tax Schedule A.*—The 1930/1 gross assessed rental is £700 less allowances for owner's rates £40 and repairs (statutory allowance) £120, making net Schedule A for year to 5th April 1931, £540. Tax payable at 4s. 6d. = £121, 10s.

due on 1st January 1931. The proportion applicable to capital
is from 5th April 1930 to 11th August 1930 (128 days)=

$\frac{128}{365}$ × £121, 10s. £42 12 2

Balance applicable to income 78 17 10

                                                        ————————
                                                        £121 10 0
                                                        ════════

(d) *Ministers' Stipend.*—The amount for crop 1930 is £5 less
tax £1, 2s. 6d. = £3, 17s. 6d., and this is assumed to refer to
the year to 11th November 1930.

The proportion applicable to capital is from 11th
   November 1929 to 11th August 1930 (273

days)=$\frac{273}{365}$ × £3, 17s. 6d. £2 18 0

Balance applicable to income 0 19 6

                                                        ————————
                                                        £3 17 6
                                                        ════════

(e) *Land Tax.*—The assessment for year to 24th March 1931
shows tax of £2, 5s. due on 1st January 1931.

The proportion applicable to capital is from
   24th March 1930 to 11th August 1930 (140

days)=$\frac{140}{365}$ × £2, 5s. £0 17 3

Balance applicable to income 1 7 9

                                                        ————————
                                                        £2 5 0
                                                        ════════

Note : Any burdens falling due before date of death are wholly
    payable by the deceased, and need not be apportioned.
    See notes on dividends " in bonis " under " Apportionment
    of Dividends " (page 52).

II. *On Purchases and Sales—*

The apportionments here are between seller and purchaser. In
addition to the price of the property the burdens for the year of sale
must all be taken into account.

Rents.—In transactions affecting farms the amount of rent to be
    apportioned depends on the terms of the agreement for sale
    and no general rule can be stated. In other cases of sales
    of property, entry is generally at a legal half-yearly term and
    no apportionment of rent is therefore necessary. If otherwise,
    the rents must be apportioned as between purchaser and
    seller on the basis of the number of days in the period applicable
    to each.

Burdens.—Assume that a house assessed at £50 is sold at Martinmas
    (11th November) 1930 for £750. The following apportionments
    are necessary :—

    (a) *Feuduty.*—This is paid half-yearly and the seller pays
        it up to Martinmas 1930. The purchaser pays future
        feuduties and so no apportionment is made.

(b) *Local Rates.*—It is known that the rates for 1930/1 will be at 10s. per £. The seller pays the purchaser the accrued rates from 15th May to 11th November 1930 (180 days) $\frac{180}{365} \times £25 = £12$, 6s. 7d.

(c) *Income Tax Schedule A.*—The net Schedule A assessment is £30 and tax for 1930/1 at 4s. 6d. thereon = £6, 15s. The seller pays the purchaser tax from 5th April to 11th November 1930 (220 days)$=\frac{220}{365} \times £6$, 15s. = £4, 1s. 4d.

Note : 15th May is frequently taken in practice as the end of the Income Tax year, for convenience, but this is not strictly correct.

III. *At End of Liferent*—

Apportionments are generally on the same basis as at the commencement of liferent. In addition, some doubt exists as to burdens paid before the date of death of the liferenter, such as insurance premiums or rates partly applicable to the period after close of the liferent. In equity these remain wholly payable out of income and no apportionment need be made, applying the " in bonis " rule to the liferenter, as at date of death of the testator (page 52).

Assume death of liferenter on 15th February 1933 and the same farms as shown above at commencement of liferent. The following apportionments are necessary :—

1. *Rents receivable due to Income*—

(a) *Blackacre :* (Pastoral farm—rent payable at legal terms). The amount of accrued rent applicable to income is from 15th May 1932 to 15th February 1933 (276 days) $= \frac{276}{365} \times £365$ = £276, less rent received at Martinmas 1932, £182, 10s. = £93, 10s.

(b) *Whiteacre :* (Arable farm—rent payable six months backhand). The amount of accrued rent applicable to income is :—

(a) Rent for half-year to 11th November 1932 (due at Whitsunday 1933) . . . £91 5 0

(b) Accrued rent from 11th November 1932 to 15th February 1933 (96 days)$=\frac{96}{365}$ $\times £182$, 10s. 48 0 0

Total accrued rent . . . £139 5 0

2. *Burdens due by Income*—

(a) *Feuduty* of £10 per annum less tax £2, 10s. = £7, 10s. p.a. The amount accrued payable applicable to income is from 11th November 1932 to 15th February 1933 (96 days)$=$ $\frac{96}{365} \times £7$, 10s. = £1, 19s. 5d.

(b) *Local Rates.*—The whole owner's rates for 1932/3, £45, were paid before death of the liferenter. If any apportionment is made it is as follows :—

Sum applicable to income—from 15th May 1932 to 15th February 1933 (276 days)$=\dfrac{276}{-\ 365}\times£45 = £34$, 0s. 6d.

Note : Applying the " in bonis " rule no apportionment is necessary.

(c) *Income Tax Schedule A.*—The tax for 1932/3 was paid on 1st January 1933—£540 at 5s. = £135. If any apportionment is made it is as follows :—

Sum applicable to income—from 5th April 1932 to 15th February 1933 (316 days)$=\dfrac{316}{365}\times£135 = £116$, 17s. 6d.

Note : Applying the " in bonis " rule no apportionment is necessary.

(d) *Ministers' Stipend.*—It is anticipated that this will amount to £5 less tax £1, 5s. = £3, 15s. for year to Martinmas 1933, and the sum applicable to income is therefore from 11th November 1932 to 15th February 1933 (96 days)$=\dfrac{96}{365}\times£3$, 15s. = 19s. 9d.

(e) *Land Tax.*—The tax for 1932/3 was paid on 1st January 1933 amounting to £2, 5s. If any apportionment is made it is as follows :—

Sum applicable to income—from 24th March 1932 to 15th February 1933 (328 days)$=\dfrac{328}{365}\times£2$, 5s. = £2, 0s. 5d.

Note : Applying the " in bonis " rule no apportionment is necessary.

CHAPTER IX

THE PREPARATION OF TRUST ACCOUNTS

PERIODICAL trust accounts are required for information of the trustees and beneficiaries. Such accounts should be prepared annually even if few transactions have taken place during the year, unless there are special reasons to the contrary, in which case a slightly longer period is admissible. The principal advantages of an annual account, compared Advantages of Annual with longer periods, are the increased simplicity of smaller statements, Accounts. the more ready explanations of transactions, the benefits of comparison, and the earlier detection of errors and defalcations. It is also convenient to ascertain frequently the exact balances due to and by liferenters which depend on the income brought out in the trust account. In judicial factories annual accounts are required.

Accounts should be prepared as at the dates of death of liferenters, and also in theory when there are changes in trustees.

The principal points to be kept in view in trust accounts are accuracy, Requirements in Accounts. simplicity, and early issue. Many trustees have no experience of accounts and it is essential that they should be clearly informed as to the funds for which they are responsible. It is frequently found in practice that non-professional men who are appointed trustees take little interest in the trust administration, and there can be little doubt that delayed and obscure accounts are partly to blame for this. Trustees should always insist on receiving proper accounts soon after the annual balancing date. If the agent makes a preliminary draft in advance of the time of closing the account, final entries can then be added and the account is easily completed soon after it is due.

Many trust accounts which are otherwise admirable fail to show the Summary. results in summarised form. The omission of a summary is fatal to the clarity of an account, except in the smallest trusts in which perhaps a single page may show the whole transactions.

The summary is not a substitute for a detailed account which is still required, and the summary should be prefixed or appended to the account so that details may readily be found.

While cash transactions comprise the main part of trust accounts Non-Cash Transactions. there may also be non-cash transactions, such as transfers of property and investments, requiring to be included in the accounts. If apportionments of income are necessary these are shown by cross-entry between capital and income, as explained in a separate chapter (page 46). The non-cash transactions occur in various circumstances of which the following are the most important. Funds are received at the beginning of the executry or trust by transfer to the executors or trustees of property and investments, in terms of the will or deed of trust, etc. Additional funds may be received as legacies or gifts to the trust, and stocks and shares in companies are sometimes received as bonuses or on reconstructions of the companies.

Funds may be distributed in settlement of specific legacies of houses, furniture or investments. Pecuniary (cash) legacies and legacies of residue may also be settled by transfer of investments for convenience.

Non-cash transactions require to be shown on both sides of the account, so that the cash balance is not affected. Funds received are added to the cash receipts and also shown as investments made, and conversely funds distributed are added to the payments and also appear as investments realised.

Cash Transactions. The original records of cash must be kept in such detail that full particulars of the transactions are available, and it is recommended that all letters and receipts be filed and arranged in order of date for reference. In large trusts a cash book and ledger should be kept, and ledger accounts should be opened for the different classes of capital and income transactions, also separate accounts for each investment showing capital and income separately as described under " English Trust Accounts " (page 74). In other cases it is sufficient if the agent keeps an account in his ledger containing details of his cash transactions on behalf of the trust, and another account for the trust bank account.

Cash may have been received or paid by sub-agents, for example, local factors of heritable property in other districts. Statements of their transactions must be obtained frequently and should be audited by the agent and incorporated in the trust account.

It is sometimes arranged for convenience that trust dividends should be remitted direct to beneficiaries, instead of being collected by the agent, and full information regarding these sums must be obtained for inclusion in the trust accounts.

Foreign Exchange. Foreign transactions settled by immediate transfer of funds to the United Kingdom are taken into account at their sterling equivalents. On the other hand if cash has been received or paid by foreign bankers and balances have been retained by them, such transactions should appear in the trust account at the exchange rates ruling on the dates when cash was received or paid. Transfers to or from the foreign account do not affect these calculations, but the remaining balance should be brought into account at the exchange rate ruling at the date of closing of the trust account, and any difference arising owing to transactions at other rates is then written off as gain or loss on exchange. As an example, the following account shows transactions on a New York bank account for year to 30th June 1933.

In such an account, where no questions of apportionment arise and there are no capital transactions, the exchange rate may be calculated for all items at the closing rate instead of bringing in each dividend, etc., at different rates. This is much simpler than the above method, but is not correct when it is necessary to apportion any foreign dividends between capital and income.

	Dollars.	Exchange Rate $=£1.	Per Accounts Sterling Equivalent.
Balance 30th June 1932 . .	$375	3·75	£100
Dividend received 1st August 1932 .	190	3·80	50
	$565		£150
Paid beneficiary 31st December 1932	320	3·20	100
Forward . .	$245		£50

Forward . .	$245		£50
Transfer to U.K. agent on ⎫ 1st March 1933 . . ⎪ (No entry in trust account ⎬ required as this is a cross ⎪ entry) ⎭	165 —— $80	3·30	50 —— Nil
Dividend received 1st April 1933	40 ——	4·00	10 ——
Balance . . .	$120		£10

The balance at 30th June 1933 was $120 at 4·80
(carried to next year) 25
————

Gain on exchange £15
————

Note.—The sterling equivalent column is purely a bookkeeping record and the balances there are not otherwise required.

As explained below, the investments are brought into each year's account at cost. In arriving at the cost figure, difficulty may arise through partial sales, new issues, reconstruction of companies, etc., and the general principles which should be observed are now described. For convenience all adjustments of the cost should be detailed in the trust accounts.

Cost of Investments.

(1) *Original Investments retained Unchanged*—

The cost to the trust is the value when received, *i.e.*, at date of testator's death in a testamentary trust, and at date of transfer in other cases.

(2) *Brokerage Expenses, Stamp Duty, and Registration Fees on Sales and Purchases*—

It is usual to add such expenses to the cost of investments purchased and deduct them from the proceeds of investments sold. Thus if £100 4% deb. stock X.Y. Co. is purchased at 80% the expenses amount to £5, 3s. (Stamp duty £1, Brokerage £4, Contract Stamp 6d. and Registration Fee 2s. 6d.) and the investment is shown at a cost of £85, 3s.

(3) *Partial Sales*—

There are two alternative methods of treating such sales, each of which ultimately produces the same result :—

(1) Proceeds of sales are set off against the cost of the total holding until (*a*) this is exhausted, or (*b*) the last share is sold (whichever first occurs) when the remainder whether profit or loss is written off. This method may result in a holding with no book cost if the proceeds of part are greater than the original cost of the whole. A minor alteration in method may be adopted by carrying the remaining holding at £1 instead of nil.

E

(2) Alternatively, the cost of the total investment may be regarded as an average figure, and the proportion applicable to the shares sold is written off on the occasion of each sale until the last instalment is written off on the final sale. For example, if half the shares are sold half the cost figure is written off.

The first method is simpler, but the second is more correct in theory, and the following example shows the effect of the two methods. Assume 1000 shares in a company cost £1800 including expenses, whereof 500 were sold in January 1932 for £2000 and the remaining 500 in September 1932 for £700 after deducting expenses in each case. The trust accounts close annually on 31st March.

Method (1)—
  Account 1931/2—

Proceeds of sale of 500 shares . . .	£2000
Cost of 1000 shares	1800
Increase on Realisation	£200

500 shares held at close of account at nil.

  Account 1932/3—

Proceeds of sale of 500 shares . . .	£700
Cost—nil	—
Increase on Realisation	£700

Note : Total increase £900.

Method (2)—
  Account 1931/2—

Proceeds of sale of 500 shares . . .	£2000
Proportion of cost of these shares : $\frac{500}{1000} \times 1800$	900
Increase on Realisation	£1100

500 shares held at close of account at £900.

  Account 1932/3—

Proceeds of sale of 500 shares . . .	£700
Proportion of cost as above	900
Decrease on Realisation	£200

Note : Net increase £900.

(4) *Additions to Existing Holdings*—

There is little advantage in showing separately in the list of investments similar shares which have been purchased at different prices or dates, so these should be merged. For example, assuming

£500 War Loan was bought in January 1931 at 101% = £505, and £500 in November 1931 at 95% = £475, including expenses in each case, the investment should appear in subsequent accounts as £1000 stock at cost of £980.

(5) *New Investments* appear at actual cost, including expenses.

(6) *Apportionment of Income*—

In theory, sums received from income account should be treated as partial realisations of the investments and deducted from the cost of the individual items. Similarly sums transferred to income account are best treated as additions to the cost of the individual investments.

The effect of the above method is to leave the total capital fund unchanged as the cash balance held on account of capital is increased or decreased correspondingly. In practice apportionments are not always shown in this way, being instead taken as additions to the capital or deductions from the capital as the case may be. This method leaves the cost of the individual investments unchanged, but while it is simpler in operation it is not strictly correct.

As an example of the two methods assume £1000 5% deb. stock X.Y. Co. was held by trustees at the close of a liferent on 13th June 1933—the last interest having been paid up to 1st April 1933, and the cost per accounts being £980, 17s. 1d. The accrued interest due to the liferenter must be transferred to income account, that is 73 days interest £10 less tax £2, 10s. = £7, 10s.

First Method—

Funds per previous account—						
£1000 5% deb. stock X.Y. Co.	.	.	.	£980	17	1
Cash balance	.	.	.	19	2	11
				£1000	0	0

Funds as at 13th June 1933—				
£1000 5% deb. stock X.Y. Co. at cost as before plus £7, 10s. accrued income now added	£988	7	1
Cash balance	11	12	11
	£1000	0	0

Second Method—

Funds per previous account as before	.	.	£1000	0 0
Funds as at 13th June 1933—				
£1000 5% deb. stock X.Y. Co. (as before)	.	£980	17	1
Cash balance	11	12	11
	£992	10	0

In an account charge and discharge, the account balances in a different way in each case. Under the first method the payment of £7, 10s. is an investment made and not separately extended into the discharge total, being added to the cost in the funds at the close of the account. Under the second method the payment is shown as a capital outlay and is extended into the discharge total.

(7) *Proceeds of Fractional Bonus Shares or Rights to New Issues*—

In strict theory these should be treated as partial realisations of the individual investments, as there is really no profit on the transaction until it is completed by sale of the investment itself. In practice these sums are frequently entered as additional funds and there is thus no need to adjust the cost of the investments.

(8) *Bonuses*—

Capital *cash bonuses* are theoretically similar to partial sales of shareholdings or fractional bonus shares and should therefore be deducted from the cost of the investment, but see (7) above as to the alternative method. *Share bonuses* do not affect the cost which should remain as before, but applied to the adjusted holding, thus : 600 ord. shares X.Z. Ltd.—being former holding of 400 shares plus 50% bonus, 200 shares = at cost (as before) £720, 3s. 8d.

(9) *Company Reconstructions*—

If two classes of shares are merged the cost figure should also be merged, as no useful purpose is served by carrying forward two separate items.

On the other hand if shares of two or more classes are issued in lieu of shares of one class, the old cost price of the total holding should become a joint-cost figure bracketed against all the shares thus :—

500 ordinary shares of £1 each fully paid ⎫
   T. Jones Ltd.   ⎬ £1107 8 8
100 deferred shares of 1s. each fully paid ⎪
   T. Jones Ltd.   ⎭

(formerly 1500 6% preference shares of £1 each fully paid).

Alternatively, it may be desired to allocate the cost between these holdings although this causes difficulty and is not recommended. For this purpose the prior security is always taken at market value leaving any balance for the junior shares. For example, assume the market value of the ordinary shares to be 7s. 6d. per share = £187, 10s.; this is taken as the cost of these shares leaving £919, 18s. 8d. (the balance) as the cost of the deferred shares irrespective of the market value. The decrease should not be written off before the date of sale.

Full details of all schemes of reconstruction should be shown in the succeeding trust account. It should be noted that shares received in lieu of dividend as distinct from bonus shares are excluded from the trust capital if liferented, as these belong to the liferenter. If they are held by the trustees on his behalf a note may be made to this effect. A recent example of such scrip dividends is provided by the issue of Brazilian Funding Bonds, to meet interest on Government Loans, when transfer of currency was impossible.

(10) *Share Sub-divisions—*

If shares are divided into two classes the cost should for simplicity be bracketed against both classes, or, if desired, an allocation of the cost may be made on the basis of market value.   (See (9).)

GENERAL NOTES ON TRUST ACCOUNTS

All accounts should be divided into classified sections—sometimes known as headings or branches—each of which is headed and numbered, and with sub-headings added where necessary. The first account commences with the funds received at the beginning of the trust, which in a testamentary trust are detailed in the Estate Duty Inventory and Corrective Inventories. All items forming part of the funds appear in the same order each year, and the income is classified with a sub-heading for each property or investment *arranged and numbered in the same order as the list of funds.* Sometimes the details are shown in a columnar statement which also serves as the list of investments. If no income is received from any investment this should be stated with a short explanation. Expenses of heritable properties are sub-headed for each block of property. *{Arrangement of Accounts.}*

In preparing a trust account it is generally advisable for simplicity to draft it and reconcile the balance without apportionments, but leaving space for these. If apportionments are required, each property and investment sub-heading in the income account is then considered individually and the calculations and cross-entries are made, followed by a further reconciliation. *{Method of Preparation.}*

Advances to residuary legatees on account of their shares should be treated as investments and included in the list of funds, as this is the best way to preserve the record of these which is required for the ultimate division of the estate. Where interest on advances is chargeable but has not been received, the amount should appear as an income receipt each year and on the other side as a further advance. *{Advances to Beneficiaries.}*

Trust accounts must always be prepared so as to conform to the terms of the trust disposition. As explained in a separate chapter (page 22) the liferenter is entitled only to the income on the trust funds. A strict division must therefore be made between capital and income if the trust is liferented, by keeping separate accounts for capital and income and making apportionments of rents and dividends, etc., unless these are specifically excluded in the trust disposition. *{Liferents.}*

If the income is not liferented (*e.g.* if held for annuitants) it is not usually necessary to draw any line of distinction between capital and income, but for convenience it is usual to separate the capital transactions except that the capital and income balances at the end of each account may be merged together.

If separate funds are directed to be held for different individual liferenters by the terms of the trust disposition, it is necessary to set aside separate investments and subsequently show the trust funds in two or more separate accounts—one for each liferented fund. In other cases, depending on circumstances, it may be sufficient to show a general fund and divide the income in the specified proportions.

All trust accounts should include a detailed list of the investments showing the cost and present value of each investment. If these are *{List of Funds.}*

E 2

numerous it is an advantage to classify them under sub-headings giving both cost and valuation sub-totals for each section.   Appropriate headings may be selected from the following list or further headings may be introduced as required :—

(1) Heritable Property.
(2) Government Stocks.
(3) Debentures and Debenture Stocks.
(4) Preference Stocks and Shares.
(5) Ordinary Stocks and Shares—Iron and Coal.
(6)   Do.   —Gas and Electrical.
(7)   Do.   —Commercial.

Summary of Accounts.   In the summary of accounts referred to above, it is desirable to give the following information :—

(1) Valuation of investments total as at close of the account and comparative figure for previous year.
(2) Reconciliation of balances in bank and in agent's hands with previous year's figures.
(3) Reconciliation of total capital of the trust at cost with previous year's account.
(4) Summary of income and reconciliation of income balances at beginning and end of year.

Account Details.   It is not correct to use the words " To " and " By " in trust accounts. Wherever possible the words " Received " and " Paid " should also be eliminated to avoid repetition.   All entries should be dated and the following details should be given :—

Interest and Dividends—
(a) Name and amount of the holding in the company.
(b) Annual rate received and whether interim or final.
(c) Period for which declared.
(d) Gross amount.
(e) Income tax deducted.
(f) Net amount.

Note : Interest is receivable on government and debenture stocks and on terminable debentures, deposits, etc.
Dividends are receivable on other investments.

Rents—
For convenience these should be shown in a rental appended to the account, thus :—
(a) Postal address of the property.
(b) Tenants' names.
(c) Annual rent.
(d) Additional charges receivable, *e.g.* insurance, or interest on improvements.
(e) Period for which receivable.
(f) Arrears of rent at beginning and end of period, stating whether anticipated to be doubtful debts.
(g) Sums actually received.
(h) Dates of expiry of leases.
(i) Alterations in rents, new leases, etc.
(j) Fire insurance.

Investments—

State the full description as on the share certificates with rate of interest or dividend (if any is fixed) and date of repayment if specified. Preference stocks and shares should be marked as non-cumulative, if appropriate. They are cumulative unless the contrary is stated. (Partick Gas Co. *v.* Taylor, 1888, 15 R. 711, and Ferguson and Forrester *v.* Buchanan, 1920, S.C. 154.)

THE STYLE OF TRUST ACCOUNTS

There are three principal styles in common use in Scotland in addition to various less orthodox combinations of these. The simplest style is the Statement of Receipts and Payments, which is appropriate for any size of trust account if completed by appending a list of investments and reconciliation of the totals. Secondly, there is the Statement of Income and Expenditure frequently adopted by charities, which is based on the former style, but also allows for outstanding items at both ends of the period. This is not suitable for testamentary trusts. Thirdly, there is the Account Charge and Discharge—a complex arrangement required in judicial factories and commonly used in other trusts, but which cannot be given unqualified recommendation under modern conditions. In practice it will be found that this name is wrongly given to many accounts which are purely cash statements. The main advantage of this style is said to be the check on accuracy through the inclusion of the funds at cost at both beginning and end of the period. While this check is of some value, errors may arise in the lists of investments in various ways.

It may also be of interest to refer to the English style of double-entry accounts although this is not in common use in Scotland.

The various styles are now described in detail.

I. STATEMENTS OF RECEIPTS AND PAYMENTS

This style of account is simply a classified cash account in which the receipts and payments are analysed under suitable headings, firstly separating the capital and income transactions, and secondly, distinguishing between the various sub-divisions of these. The account is incomplete if it does not also include a list of the investments at the close of the period showing the cost and present value of each. There should be appended reconciliations with the previous account of the totals of investments and capital and income cash balances, as shown in examples below. In order to reconcile the investments when there have been realisations during the year it is necessary to compare the cost and proceeds of each.

Example—

Investments at beginning at cost—

£200 3½% War Loan .	.	.	£196 13 2
£100 4% Victory Bond	.	.	94 3 0
			£290 16 2

The Victory Bond was repaid at par during the year = £100, giving an increase over cost of £5, 17s., and there was invested £90 in a debenture of the Aberdonian Investment Company.

Investments at close of account at cost—

£200 3½% War Loan	.	.	.	.	£196	13	2
£90 4% deb. Aberdonian Investment Co.					90	0	0

	£286	13	2
Add Cash Balance . . .	10	0	0

	£296	13	2

Reconciliation—

Funds at beginning	.	.	.	.	£290	16	2
Add Increase on Realisation			.		5	17	0

Funds at end	.	.	.	.	£296	13	2

Further particulars are shown in examples later (pages 76 to 82).

II. Statements of Income and Expenditure

This style is also based on the classified cash account, *but takes into account outstanding sums*—whether receivable or payable—at both ends of the period. The income thus consists of sums received plus items receivable at the close of the period, less sums receivable at the beginning of the period, thus giving net actual earnings for the year. Expenditure is treated similarly.

It is usual to append a balance sheet in common form showing all assets and liabilities as at the close of the year, including the income balance in the same way as a profit and loss account balance. The income summary for publication to subscribers to the charity is generally prepared in the profit and loss account style, with income on the right and expenditure on the left.

III. Accounts Charge and Discharge

The principle of these accounts is that the agent charges himself with funds at the beginning of the period plus receipts, and discharges on the other side an equal sum made up of payments plus funds remaining at the close of the period. In this style it must be noted that investments realised are excluded from the receipts as they are already included in the charge by forming part of the funds at the beginning, but differences due to increases or decreases on realisation are brought in to charge and discharge respectively. Similarly, investments made are not included in the payments as they are shown in the discharge by forming part of the funds at close of the period.

Further particulars of these and other difficulties are now given :—

I. *Estate Realised—*

As all the trust funds are already included in the charge by forming part of the funds at the commencement of period (Charge Branch I.) the proceeds of realisation are excluded, but any increase or decrease on realisation is included in the charge or discharge. The usual procedure is to show the estate realised in an inner column which is not included in the sum of the charge, being merely a note, and from this the increases and decreases are ascertained in either of the following ways :—

   (a) By entering in a further column the cost of all items realised and comparing the total realised with this figure, showing in one sum the net increase or decrease over the whole period.

   (b) By subtracting the relative cost of each item realised giving an increase or decrease on each item, which are entered in additional columns for increase and decrease. These columns are then totalled and set off against each other to ascertain the net result. Both methods give the same result, but the latter method is recommended as being clearer.

II. *Estate Invested*—

As the new investments are included in the sum of the discharge by inclusion in the funds as at close of the account, these must be excluded from the payments forming part of the discharge. This is effected by showing the estate invested in an inner column which is not extended. It is not advisable to omit the heading altogether although this is sometimes done.

III. *Advances to Beneficiaries on Account of Residue*—

Such advances form part of the funds at close of the account (in the same way as estate invested) and must not be included again in the sum of the discharge. They are shown in an inner column which is not extended.

IV. *Bank Transactions*—

Bank balances are shown as part of the trust funds at each end of the period, and all sums drawn and lodged should be omitted altogether from the account, as this does not affect the reconciliation and they are of no interest.

V. *Revaluation of Estate*—

As an alternative to the correct basis of including investments at the same (cost) figure in the list of funds each year, they are sometimes revalued each year and the increase or decrease on revaluation is added to the charge or discharge respectively. This is not recommended as it does not preserve a record of the actual cost of each investment and is more complicated in operation. When the trust is to be wound up the last account should, however, include a revaluation.

As explained elsewhere (page 69) it is advisable to make a valuation of the investments, but this is only an appendix and does not form part of the account charge and discharge.

VI. *Liferents as affecting Accounts*—

Where there is a liferent of the trust funds there should be a division of the account so that there are a capital charge and discharge and an income charge and discharge, as this is simpler than merging them all together. In this case the income bank and cash balances at beginning and end are excluded from the funds in the capital account, and appear in income charge and discharge respectively. The capital and income cash balances must together equal the net cash balance per the agents' books, and similarly for bank balances.

VII. *Rents*—

The amount of rents included in the charge should be the total falling due and not the sum actually received, but arrears are included in the funds at both ends. Bad debts should be deducted from the total falling due. If there is a separate income account (see VI. above) all these items are shown there.

Example—
Charge—
1. *Included in Funds at beginning of period*
Rents in arrear at this date £20
2. *Included in Income of period*
Rents receivable (less bad debts written off) . 200

—————
£220
═════

Discharge—
Included in Funds at end of period
Rents in arrear at this date £15

The difference between sums in the charge and discharge, £205, represents sums received, and thus reconciles with the addition to the cash balance.

An alternative method, sometimes adopted, is to bring into income the actual cash received, and show arrears in a note. This is not strictly correct, but is simpler than the other method.

VIII. *Partnerships and Trading Profits*—

The actual earnings of the period as shown by the accounts of the business are included in the income, not the sums drawn out of the business, in the same way as rents. The detailed trading accounts are sometimes appended to the trust account. The capital and accumulated profits are included in the funds at each end of the period, and the difference between profits earned and drawings is shown in the accounts by changes in the accumulated profits figure.

IX. *Judicial Factories*—

The account must include all the usual particulars described above, and in addition an account-current must be appended showing all transactions including bank transactions and closing with the cash balance shown in the Account Charge and Discharge. Accounts must be prepared annually, and signed by the factor, then lodged for audit with the Accountant of Court along with vouchers arranged and numbered. The factor is remunerated by commission fixed by the Accountant of Court.

IV. ENGLISH STYLE

In this style there is required a set of double-entry books consisting of cash-book, journal and ledger. At the beginning a ledger account is opened called estate account (or corpus account) which is credited by journal entry with the whole assets and debited with any liabilities, such as debts due by deceased. In executries this account should bring out the amount per estate duty inventory as the balance after the opening entries are made. Corresponding entries appear on the other side in accounts for (assets) investments, bank current account, heritable property, and (liabilities) debts due by deceased, etc. The investments account may conveniently be in the form of a control account, and if so a separate investment ledger is required in which there are accounts for the individual investments, showing details of the holdings and the cost (or inventory value) of each, which in total should agree with the control account. A second control account, for income on investments, reconciles with the total of the income balances appearing in the separate accounts for the various investments. In the investment ledger it will be found convenient to have a page for each investment showing income on one part of the page and the capital transactions on another part. The income balances are closed off by transfer to general revenue account annually.

Profits and losses on realisation are transferred from investments to estate account after sales are made. Apportionments may be shown by journal entry from investments account to income on investments account, or alternatively the original cash book entry is made in two parts—one crediting each of these accounts.

Payments are charged to accounts for government duties, debts due by deceased, legacies, annuities, management, etc. At the end of the year all these accounts are closed off by transfer to capital expenditure account, or revenue expenditure account, as the case may be. Subsequently these accounts are in turn transferred to capital account and general revenue account. The free income is transferred to the credit of the liferenter.

The cash book is preferably ruled with capital and income columns as this shows separate balances for each, but in practice it must be remembered that it is frequently necessary to make transfers from capital to income account, for example, for apportionments omitted or wrongly calculated. Bank columns are also required unless every transaction is direct to or from the bank account, in which case the balance on the cash book is the balance in bank, subject to outstanding cheques.

The trust account at the end of the year consists of the estate account, capital expenditure account, revenue expenditure account, general revenue account, and balance sheet, and there should be appended a schedule of investment ledger balances—both capital and income— reconciled with the totals per balance sheet and revenue account. The present valuation of the investments may be noted on the schedule.

CHAPTER X

SPECIMEN TRUST ACCOUNTS

Specimen Executry Account of Receipts and Payments.

EXECUTRY OF THE LATE ALEXANDER JOHN MURRAY

SUMMARY OF ACCOUNTS from 11th January 1932 (date of death)
to 30th September 1932 (close of executry)

		£	s.	d.
Estate Realised		£375	10	
Add Income Received		16	3	
Miscellaneous Receipt			7	
		£392	2	

	£	s.	d.			
Less Debts due by Deceased	£9	11	5			
Deathbed and Funeral Expenses	10	16	6			
Government Duties and Interest thereon . .	89	16	4			
Legacy	100	0	0			
Income Tax	1	17	6			
Management	18	10	6			
				230	12	

	£	s.
Cash balance payable to Miss Elizabeth Murray as residuary legatee	£161	9
Add Value of investments transferred to her as at 15th July 1932 .	659	10
Total Residue of Estate	£820	19

STATEMENT OF RECEIPTS AND PAYMENTS by Thomas Murray, W.
as Agent for the Executors of the late ALEXANDER JO
MURRAY.
From 11th January 1932 (date of death)
To 30th September 1932 (close of executry).

RECEIPTS

Note of Values as at Date of Death.						
£ s. d.	I. ESTATE REALISED :—					
	1932.					
£82 10 3	Feb. 10. Received sum at credit of current account with Bank of Scotland				£82	10
21 0 0	„ 15. Proceeds of 20 National Savings Certificates . .				21	8
50 0 0	Mar. 20. Uplifted Deposit Receipt with Bank of Scotland dated 6th October 1931				50	0
202 0 0	Apl. 15. Received proceeds of £200 5% War Loan 1929-47 at 98½ less expenses				194	15
27 10 0	June 10. Received proceeds of household furniture sold by auction				23	5
3 11 8	„ 24. Income tax recovered to date of death . .				3	11
					£375	10
	II. INCOME RECEIVED :—					
	1932.					
0 15 0	Mar. 20. Interest on Deposit Receipt with Bank of Scotland p. £50 dated 6th October 1931	£0	18	10		
£387 6 11						
	Forward	£0	18	10	£375	10

RECEIPTS—(*Continued*).   Forward | £375 | 10 | 11

	£	s.	d.
II. INCOME RECEIVED—(*continued*) Forward	£0	18	10
1932.			
Mar. 21. Imperial Chemical Industries, Ltd., ½ yr's div. on 200 7% pref. shares of £1 each fully paid, to 31st December 1931 £7 less tax at 5s. 6d. (adjusting previous tax rate) £1, 18s. 6d.	5	1	6
(This div. was due on 1st Feb. 1932.)			
June 1. ½ yr's int. on £300 5% War Loan 1929-1947 (no tax deducted) . . .	7	10	0
July 1. Lever Brothers, Ltd., ½ yr's div. to 30th June on £100 7% pref. stock £3, 10s. less tax at 4s. 9d. 16s. 7d. . .	2	13	5
Note (1) Subsequent dividends are payable direct to Miss Elizabeth Murray.			
(2) *Author's Note only*: When there are few dividends as in this case it is not necessary to show sub-headings for each investment on which income should be receivable.			
III. MISCELLANEOUS :—	16	3	9
1932.			
June 15. Received rebate on insurance premium on furniture	0	7	6
TOTAL RECEIPTS	£392	2	2

PAYMENTS

					£	s.	d.
DEBTS DUE BY DECEASED :—							
1932.							
Jan. 15. John Wilson, Grocer					£1	8	2
James Smith, Butcher					0	15	6
Feb. 28. Burgh Consolidated Rates (on house occupied) 1931-32 . .					2	7	9
May 15. ½ yr's rent of house to date					5	0	0
Note.—Part of this rent applies to period after death, but the house could not be sub-let and the rent was not subject to rebate on vacating occupation before Whitsunday.							
					£9	11	5

	£	s.	d.		£	s.	d.
DEATHBED AND FUNERAL EXPENSES :—							
1932.							
Jan. 15. Dr Johnson—fee for professional services . . .	£1	11	6				
„ 28. McGregor & Co., Undertakers, for funeral . . .	7	10	0				
Feb. 20. James Duncan—for inscription on tombstone . . .	1	15	0				
					10	16	6

	£	s.	d.		£	s.	d.
GOVERNMENT DUTIES AND INTEREST THEREON :—							
1932.							
Jan. 31. Estate Duty 3% on £1050	£31	10	0				
Interest thereon	0	1	4				
Feb. 7. Dues of Confirmation	5	0	0				
„ 28. Legacy Duty 10% on £100 legacy to Mrs Whytock .	10	0	0				
July 31. Legacy Duty 5% on £865 residue of estate . .	43	5	0				
					89	16	4

					£	s.	d.
LEGACY :—							
1932.							
Feb. 28. Mrs Isabella Whytock					100	0	0
Note.—Personal effects (valued at £5) were handed to Mrs Whytock as instructed in Will.							
Forward					£210	4	3

PAYMENTS—(*Continued*).   Forward | £210 | 4

V. INCOME TAX :—
   Sum reserved to meet tax on £7, 10s. War Loan Interest received 1st June
   1932 (at 5s.) . . . .   1 | 17

VI. MANAGEMENT :—
    1932.

	£ s. d.		
Feb. 10. John Edgar—fee for valuation of personal effects and furniture	£0	10	6
Mar. 15. Registration fee of Confirmation—Lever Brothers, Ltd.	0	2	6
„ 20. Registration fee of Confirmation—Imperial Chemical Industries, Ltd.	0	2	6
July 15. Stamp on transfer of Lever Brothers stock to residuary legatee—Miss Murray	0	10	0
Stamp on transfer of Imperial Chemical Industries shares to residuary legatee—Miss Murray .	0	10	0
Registration fee of transfer Lever Brothers, Ltd..	0	2	6
Registration fee of transfer Imperial Chemical Industries Ltd.	0	2	6
Sept. 30. Thomas Murray, W.S., Business Account for preparation of Estate Duty Account, payment of duty, realisation of estate, payment of debts and legacy, etc., and transfer of residue—restricted to . . .	16	0	0
Thomas Murray, W.S., posts and outlays . .	0	10	0

18 | 1(

TOTAL PAYMENTS . . . . . | £230 | 1:

CASH SUMMARY

Receipts	£392	?
Less Payments	230	1:
Balance payable to deceased's sister—Miss Elizabeth Murray—as residuary legatee	£161	(

Note of Values as at Date of Death.	The following investments have also been transferred to Miss Murray—valued as at 15th July 1932 :—		
£303 0 0	1. £300 5% War Loan 1929-47 at 101½	£304	1(
125 0 0	2. £100 7% pref. stock Lever Brothers, Ltd., at 24s. . . .	120	(
237 10 0	3. 200 7% pref. shares of £1 each fully paid Imperial Chemical Industries, Ltd., at 23s. 6d.	235	(
£665 10 0		£659	1(

Note.—The estate at date of death per Confirmation amounted to £1052, 16s. 11d., wh
   £387, 6s. 11d. is included in estate realised, and the balance is £665, 10s., as stated a

*Specimen Account—(with Liferent of Trust Income)—
Receipts and Payments Style*

WILLIAM McGREGOR'S TRUST

SUMMARY OF ACCOUNTS for year to 31st December 1932

CAPITAL.

Estate as at close of last account (at cost)	£1032	7	3
Add Increase on Realisation	12	11	10
	£1044	19	1
Less Management Expenses proportion	2	2	0
Estate as at close of this account (at cost)	£1042	17	1

The present value of the trust funds is £899, 19s. 10d., compared
with £847, 6s. in 1931—an increase of £52, 13s. 10d.

INCOME.

Rents Received				£80	0	0
Add Dividends Received				21	13	2
				£101	13	2
Less Burdens on Heritable Property . . .	£30	2	6			
Repairs to Heritable Property . . .	20	6	5			
Annuity paid	7	10	0			
Management Expenses proportion . . .	8	2	0			
Income Tax	3	15	0			
				69	15	11
Free Income for year				£31	17	3
Add Balance of Income per last account				11	7	6
				£43	4	9
Less Payments to Mrs McGregor—the liferentrix . . .				31	7	6
Balance of Income as at close of this account . . .				£11	17	3

	Capital.			Income.		
CASH :—						
Balance in hands of agent as at close of last account	£15	10	0	£11	7	6
Add Capital Receipts	188	1	10			
Income Receipts				101	13	2
	£203	11	10	£113	0	8
Less Capital Payments	202	2	0			
Income Payments				101	3	5
Balance in hands of agent as at close of this account	£1	9	10	£11	17	3

TRUST ACCOUNTANCY

STATEMENT OF RECEIPTS AND PAYMENTS by Thomas Murray, W
as Agent for the Trustees of the late WILLIAM McGREGOR.

From 31st December 1931
To 31st December 1932.

CAPITAL RECEIPTS

1932.

June 10. Received proceeds of £200 4% Funding Loan 1960-90 at
95% less expenses . . . . . . | £188 | 15

Author's Note.—The contract date is taken here as the sale was
for cash settlement (although the proceeds were not received
until 18th June) according to rules of apportionment.

Less Interest accrued from 1st May to 10th June 1932 included in
price, but applicable to income (40 days) 17s. 6d., less tax 4s. 4d. | 0 | 13

| | £188 | 1 | 10 | £188 | 1 |

Note.—Cost of stock per last account . . 175 10 0

Increase on Realisation . . . £12 11 10

TOTAL CAPITAL RECEIPTS . . . . | £188 | 1

CAPITAL PAYMENTS

I. INVESTMENT MADE :—

1932.

June 20. Placed on deb. with Aberdonian Investment
Company at 5% for 3 years . . . . | £200 | 0

II. MANAGEMENT :—

1932.

Dec. 31. Thomas Murray, W.S., fee for capital transactions
during year including above investments and
preparation of this account . . . . | 2 | 2

TOTAL CAPITAL PAYMENTS . . . . | £202 | 2

INCOME RECEIPTS

I. RENTS per Appendix . . . . | £80 | 0

II. INTEREST AND DIVIDENDS :—

1. *On £300 5% War Loan 1929-47 now £300 3½% War Loan.*

1932.

June 1. ½ yr's int. (no tax deducted) . . | £7 | 10 | 0
July 18. Bonus of 1% on conversion . . | 3 | 0 | 0
Dec. 1. ½ yr's int. (no tax deducted) . . | 7 | 10 | 0

Note.—This stock has now been converted | £18 | 0 | 0
into 3½% stock.

2. *On £200 4% Funding Loan 1960-90.*

1932.

May 1. ½ yr's int. to date £4 less tax £1 | £3 | 0 | 0
June 10. Accrued int. to date of sale per
Capital Receipts 17s. 6d. less
tax 4s. 4d. . . . | 0 | 13 | 2

| | | 3 | 13 | 2

Note.—This stock was sold during year.

Forward | £21 | 13 | 2 | £80 | 0

INCOME RECEIPTS—(*Continued*)	Forward			£80	0	0

II. INTEREST AND DIVIDENDS—(*continued*). Forward	£21	13	2			
3. *On* £200 5% *deb. Aberdonian Investment Co., Ltd.* No interest yet received. The first interest is due on 1st January 1933. This debenture was taken up on 20th June 1932.						
				21	13	2
TOTAL INCOME RECEIPTS				£101	13	2

INCOME PAYMENTS

I. BURDENS ON HERITABLE PROPERTY—36-40 MEADOW WALK, EDINBURGH :—					
1932.					
Feb. 28. Local Consolidated Rates 1931-2—Owner . .			£11	10	0
May 15. ½ yr's feuduty £1, 10s. less tax 7s. 6d. . . .			1	2	6
Nov. 11. Do. Do. . .			1	2	6
Insurance premium on comprehensive policy .			3	17	6
Dec. 31. Income Tax Schedule A, 1932-3			12	10	0
			£30	2	6

II. REPAIRS TO HERITABLE PROPERTY :—							
1932.							
Mar. 31. John Simpson, Painter . . .	£12	6	6			
July 15. William Dunbar, Plumber . .	1	14	7			
Sept. 30. Do. . .	1	18	1			
Nov. 15. John McAllister, Slater . . .	4	7	3			
				20	6	5

III. ANNUITY :—					
1932.					
May 15. George McGregor annuity for year to date £10 less tax £2, 10s.			7	10	0

IV. MANAGEMENT :—							
1932.							
Dec. 31. Thomas Murray, W.S., commission, etc., for year to date—restricted to . .	£7	7	0			
Thomas Murray, W.S., posts and bank charges	0	15	0			
				8	2	0

V. INCOME TAX :—					
1932.					
Dec. 31. Income Tax Schedule D, 1932-3, on War Loan interest £15 at 5s.			3	15	0

VI. PAYMENTS TO LIFERENTRIX—MRS McGREGOR :—							
1932.							
Jan. 31. Per British Linen Bank—balance per last account	£11	7	6			
Feb. 28. Do. —for quarter .	5	0	0			
May 31. Do. Do.	5	0	0			
Aug. 31. Do. Do.	5	0	0			
Nov. 30. Do. Do.	5	0	0			
				31	7	6
TOTAL INCOME PAYMENTS				£101	3	5

F

TRUST ACCOUNTANCY

RENTAL OF PROPERTY for year to 31st December 1932

Address.	Tenants.	Annual Rent.	Period due.	Arrears at beginning.	Sums Received.	Arrears at end.	Note
36 Meadow Walk (Shop)	J. Mackay	£20 0 0	Year to Marts. 1932	...	£20 0 0	...	
38 Meadow Walk	A. Baillie	12 0 0	Year to 1st Jan. 1933	£0 10 6	11 7 6	£1 3 0	Paya mont in advar
Do.	T. McGregor	9 0 0	Do.	1 0 0	10 0 0	...	Do
Do.	J. Dalkeith	10 0 0	Do.	...	9 15 0	0 5 0	Do
Do.	W. Nelson	11 10 0	Do.	1 10 0	10 0 0	3 0 0	Do
40 Meadow Walk (Shop)	Miss Johnston	20 0 0	Year to Marts. 1932	...	18 17 6	1 2 6	
		£82 10 0		£3 0 6	£80 0 0	£5 10 6	

Insurance of the property is covered by comprehensive policy p. £500 with XY. Co. (pren £3, 17s. 6d.).

Note.—Rents Receivable . . . £82 10 0
Add Arrears at beginning . 3 0 6

£85 10 6
Less Cash Received . . 80 0 0

Arrears at end . . . £5 10 6

VALUATION OF TRUST FUNDS as at 31st December 1932

	Cost.			Present Price.	Present V	
Heritable Property 36-40 Meadow Walk, Edinburgh .	£550	0	0	say	£400	
£300 3½% War Loan	291	7	3	99½	298	1
£200 5% deb. Aberdonian Investment Co., Ltd., due 20th June 1935	200	0	0	say par	200	
Capital Balance at credit with Agent . . .	1	9	10		1	
	£1042	17	1		£899	1

Note.—There is a balance of income at credit with Agent of £11, 17s. 3d. and arrears of outstanding of £5, 10s. 6d.

THE BENEVOLENT INSTITUTION

SUMMARY OF ACCOUNTS for year to 31st December 1932

INCOME ACCOUNT.

Expenditure.	£	s.	d.	Income.	£	s.	d.
1. Expenses of Property occupied by Beneficiaries	39	7	6	1. Income from Investments	530	0	0
2. Annuities to Beneficiaries	261	8	6	2. Subscriptions from Members	43	5	0
3. Special Payments to Beneficiaries	108	10	0	3. Donations from Members	5	7	6
4. Inspector's Salary and Expenses	20	0	0				
5. Management Expenses—including Staff Salaries and Office Expenses	85	7	6				
	514	13	6				
Surplus Income for year	63	19	0				
	£578	12	6		£578	12	6

BALANCE SHEET as at 31st December 1932.

Assets.					£	s.	d.	Liabilities.					£	s.	d.
I. Cash in Bank					73	18	3	I. Expenses of Property accrued					14	10	0
II. Income accrued on Investments					152	6	6	II. Annuities accrued					2	2	9
III. Subscriptions unpaid					0	10	0	III. Capital Reserve:—							
IV. Income Tax Recoverable					65	0	0	Per last Account	£7350	0	0				
V. Investments (at cost)					10,478	10	0	Add Legacies received during year	75	0	0		7,425	0	0
Note.—The present value of the Investments is £13,500.								IV. Income Surplus:—							
VI. Heritable Property—Land and Buildings:—								Per last Account	£4512	5	6				
Per last Account	£1163	15	0					Add Surplus for year	63	19	0		4,576	4	6
Add Price of land purchased and improvements to property during year	83	17	6		1,247	12	6								
					£12,017	17	3						£12,017	17	3

COMPUTATION of certain items of Income and Expenditure for above accounts of THE BENEVOLENT INSTITUTION for yea 31st December 1932. (Not shown in published accounts.)

INCOME

I. INCOME FROM INVESTMENTS :—

1. *On £3000 4% Funding Loan—*
1932.

May 1. ½ yr's int. to date £60 less tax £15	.	.	.	£45
Nov. 1. Do. Do.	.	.	.	45
				£90

2. *On £10,000 4% Victory Bonds—*
1932.

Mar. 1. ½ yr's int. £200 less tax at 5s. 6d. (correcting 6d. in previous deduction) £55	£145 0 0			
Sept. 1. Do. tax at 5s., £50 . .	150 0 0			
				295
				£385
Add Sum at credit of income tax account				145
				£530

Note.—The amount of accrued income as at 31st December 1932 was the same as at 31st December 1931 (£152, 6s. 6d.) as detailed below :—

On £3000 4% Funding Loan from 1st November to 31st December 1932 (60 days)	£19	1
On £10,000 4% Victory Bonds from 1st September to 31st December 1932 (121 days)	132	1
	£152	

IA. INCOME TAX :—
1932.

Apl. 20. Sum recovered in respect of year to 5th April 1932 .	£135	
May 15. Tax deducted on payment of feuduty £10 at 5s. .	2	1
(This is paid over to Inland Revenue by set-off against claim.)	£137	1

Add Sum recoverable as at 31st December 1932—

(1) On 4% Funding Loan interest received 1st November 1932	£15 0 0		
(2) On 4% Victory Bond interest received 1st September 1932	50 0 0		
			65
			£202
Less Sum recoverable as at 31st December 1931 per last Balance Sheet			57
Total at credit of account transferred to Income from Investments Account			£145

INCOME—(*Continued*)

II. Subscriptions :—

Sums received during year	£44	10	0
Add Sums outstanding as at 31st December 1932 . . .	0	10	0
	£45	0	0
Less Do. Do. 1931 . . .	1	15	0
	£43	5	0

EXPENDITURE

I. Expenses of Property occupied by Beneficiaries :—

1932.

Jan. 31. Local Consolidated Rates 1931-2—Owner and Occupier	£25	10	0
May 15. Year's feuduty	10	0	0
Note.—Income Tax was deducted on payment and this is included in Income Br. I.			
June 10. James Brown, Painter	3	5	0
	£38	15	0
Add Accrued expenses at 31st December 1932 (estimated) .	14	10	0
	£53	5	0
Less Accrued expenses at 31st December 1931 per last Balance Sheet	13	17	6
Net expenditure for year . . .	£39	7	6

Note.—No rents are receivable from beneficiaries.

II. Annuities to Beneficiaries :—

Actual payments during year (10 annuitants at 10s. per week for 52 weeks)	£260	0	0
Add 3 days' annuities outstanding at 31st December 1932 .	2	2	9
	£262	2	9
Less 1 day's annuities Do. 1931 .	0	14	3
	£261	8	6

III. Special Payments to Beneficiaries :—

1932.

July 15. Miss Maxwell—gift on 80th birthday . . .	£5	0	0
Sept. 10. Miss Dryburgh—allowance for medical attention .	3	10	0
Dec. 25. Christmas allowance of £10 to each annuitant . .	100	0	0
	£108	10	0

IV. Inspector's Salary and Expenses :—

1932.

Dec. 31. James Nelson—allowance for year	£20	0	0

V. Management Expenses :—

1932.

Dec. 31. William Robertson—amount of salary as treasurer for year	£50	0	0
William Robertson—Clerk's salary (part time) . .	26	0	0
Do. Allowance for stationery . . .	6	15	0
Do. Postages, etc.	2	12	6
	£85	7	6

F 2

TRUST ACCOUNTANCY

INCOME CASH SUMMARY for year 1932

RECEIPTS :—				£	s.
Dividends received				£385	0
Income tax recovered				137	10
Subscriptions				44	10
Donations				5	7
				£572	7
Less PAYMENTS :—					
Expenses of Property	£38	15	0		
Annuities to Beneficiaries	260	0	0		
Special Payments to Beneficiaries	108	10	0		
Inspector's Salary and Expenses	20	0	0		
Management	85	7	6		
				512	12
Income Cash Surplus for year				£59	15

RECONCILIATION OF INCOME AND EXPENDITURE ACCOUNT

	1931.			1932.	
OUTSTANDING INCOME :—					
Income tax	£57	10	0	£65	0
Interest on Investments	152	6	6	152	6
Subscriptions	1	15	0	0	10
	£211	11	6	£217	16
				211	11
INCREASE IN OUTSTANDING INCOME				£6	5
OUTSTANDING EXPENDITURE :—					
Expenses of Property	£13	17	6	£14	10
Annuities	0	14	3	2	2
	£14	11	9	£16	12
				14	11
INCREASE IN LIABILITIES				£2	
Increase in Assets				£6	5
Cash Surplus				59	15
				£66	
Less Increase in Liabilities				2	
NET IMPROVEMENT				£63	15

Specimen Account Charge and Discharge

TRUST OF THE LATE ALEXANDER MURRAY

SUMMARY OF ACCOUNTS for year to 31st December 1931

I. CAPITAL :—

(a) Amount of Funds and cash balance per last Account (at cost) — £2883 17 0

Add Additional Funds—Legacy from the late Mrs Annie Murray — 100 0 0

£2983 17 0

Less Estate Duty	£5	0	0	
Management—proportion	1	3	6	
			6	3 6

Amount of Funds and cash balance at close of account (at cost) . . . . £2977 | 13 | 6

(b) *Reconciliation Note.*—The investments (excluding cash) per last account £2877 13 4

Add Investments made 180 6 2

£3057 19 6

Less Investments realised 2 10 0

Investments (excluding cash) at close of account (at cost) . £3055 9 6

(c) The present value of the total funds is £3048 compared with £3200 in 1930.

II. INCOME :—

Income Received £204 12 2

Less Management—proportion 7 12 6

Free Income for year £196 19 8

Add Balance at close of last account 18 7 6

£215 7 2

Less Paid to Liferentrix 140 0 0

Balance at close of this Account . . . £75 7 2

ACCOUNT CHARGE AND DISCHARGE of the Intromission
Thomas Murray, W.S., as Agent for the Trustees of the
ALEXANDER MURRAY.

For year to 31st December 1931.

CAPITAL CHARGE

I. ESTATE AS AT CLOSE OF LAST ACCOUNT AT COST :—			
1. £1000 4% deb. stock XX, Ltd.		£742	13
2. 500 6% partic. pref. shares of £1 each fully paid XX, Ltd.		485	0
3. Share of capital of the partnership of Murray & Murray, Iron-mongers, Edinburgh, including undrawn profits . .		1500	0
4. Advances to Frederick T. Murray on account of residue .		150	0
5. Capital Balance at credit with Agent		6	3
		£2883	17
II. ADDITIONAL FUNDS RECEIVED :—			
1931.			
June 30. Legacy from the late Mrs Annie Murray, deceased's grandmother (free of legacy duty) . . .		100	0
Note.—This legacy was vested in the deceased, but was not payable until the death of deceased's last surviving sister. No estate duty was paid on this legacy at the time of testator's death. For payment, see Capital Discharge I.			

III. INVESTMENT REALISED :—
1931.
May 18. Received proceeds of rights to 10 new ord.
shares of £1 each XX, Ltd., at 6s. 3d.
market premium less expenses .   £2 10 0

Note.—Cost of 500 6% partic. pref. shares
per Br. I., 2 . . . .   £485 0 0
Deduct above receipt . .   2 10 0

Cost of 500 6% partic. pref. shares
now converted into 500 6% cum.
pref. (non-partic.) and 50 ord.
shares all of £1 each fully paid, per
Funds at close of account .   £482 10 0

SUM OF CAPITAL CHARGE		£2983	17

CAPITAL DISCHARGE

I. ESTATE DUTY :—			
1931.			
Aug. 10. Additional Estate Duty at 5% on £100 legacy received per Cap. Charge II.		£5	0
Forward		£5	0

CAPITAL DISCHARGE—(*Continued*)				Forward	£5	0	0

II. INVESTMENTS MADE :—

1. 4% *Victory Bonds* :—

1931.

July 10. Paid for £50 Bond at 96% and expenses				£48	15	0	
Less amount of accrued interest included in price transferred from Income Charge II., 5, from 1st March to 10th July 1931 (131 days) 14s. 4d. less tax 3s. 7d.				0	10	9	
Cost of £50 Bond per Funds at close of Account				£48	4	3	

2. *Advances to Frederick T. Murray* :—

1931.

June 30. Further advance .	£50	0	0					
Dec. 31. Interest on advances due per Income Charge II., 4, unpaid and added to capital sum due by him . . .	6	11	5					
				56	11	5		

Note.—Advances p. Capital Charge I., 4 . . .	£150	0	0	
Add above sums . .	56	11	5	
Advances p. Funds at close of account . .	£206	11	5	

3. *Share of partnership capital of Murray & Murray* :—

1931.

Dec. 31. Amount of undrawn profits for year to date				75	10	6	

Note.

(1) Share of profits per Income Charge II., 3 . .	£135	10	6	
Less sums drawn during year	60	0	0	
Balance as above . .	£75	10	6	

(2) Amount of capital plus undrawn profits per Capital Charge I., 3 . .	£1500	0	0	
Add above sum . .	75	10	6	
Amount per Funds at close of Account . . .	£1575	10	6	

		£180	6	2	

		Forward	£5	0	0	

CAPITAL DISCHARGE—(*Continued*) Forward £5 0

III. MANAGEMENT :—

1931.
Dec. 31. Thomas Murray, W.S., commission, etc.,
for year . . . . . . £1 | 1 | 0
Thomas Murray, posts, etc. . . . 0 | 2 | 6

1 | 3

IV. ESTATE AS AT CLOSE OF THIS ACCOUNT AT COST :—

Present
Value.

£800	1. £1000 4% deb. stock XX, Ltd. . .	£742	13	4
	2. 500 6% cum. pref. shares of £1 each fully ⎫			
475	paid XX, Ltd. . . . . ⎬	482	10	0
20	3. 50 ord. shares of £1 each fully paid Do. ⎭			
	4. Share of Capital of the partnership of			
	Murray & Murray, Ironmongers, Edin-			
1576	burgh, including undrawn profits .	1575	10	6
	5. Advances to Frederick T. Murray on			
207	account of residue . . .	206	11	5
48	6. £50 4% Victory Bond . . .	48	4	3
£3126		£3055	9	6
78	*Less* Capital Balance due to Agent . .	77	16	0
£3048			2977	13

SUM OF CAPITAL DISCHARGE Equal to CHARGE . £2983 | 17

INCOME CHARGE

I. INCOME BALANCE at credit with Agent as at close of last Account £18 | 7

II. INTEREST AND DIVIDENDS RECEIVED :—
1. *On £1000 4% deb. stock XX, Ltd.*

1931.
Mar. 31. ½ yr's int. to date £20 less tax at 4s. 6d.,
£4, 10s. . . . . . £15 | 10 | 0
Sept. 30. ½ yr's int. to date £20 less tax at 5s., £5 15 | 0 | 0

£30 | 10 | 0

2. *On 500 6% partic. pref. shares of £1 each fully
paid XX, Ltd.*—
1931.
Feb. 28. Yr's div. for 1930 of 8% £40 less tax
at 4s. 6d., £9 . . . . . 31 | 0 | 0
Note.—These shares have been exchanged for
500 non-partic. 6% pref. shares and 50 ord.
shares per Capital Charge III.
2a. *On 50 ord. shares of £1 each fully paid XX, Ltd.*—
These shares were received during year per
Capital Charge III.
No dividend yet received.
3. *Share of profits of partnership of Murray &
Murray*—
1931.
Dec. 31. Share of profits earned for year 1931 135 | 10 | 6

Forward £197 | 0 | 6 | £18 | 7

INCOME CHARGE—*(Continued)*   Forward   £18 | 7 | 6

II. INTEREST AND DIVIDENDS RECEIVED—*(continued)*

Forward				£197	0	6			

4. *On advances on account of residue to Frederick T. Murray at 5%—*

1931.

Dec. 31. Yr's int. to date on sums advanced per last account —£150 . . . . £7 | 10 | 0

Int. to date on £50 advanced on 30th June 1931 (184 days)   1 | 5 | 2

       £8 | 15 | 2

Less tax at 5s.   .   .   .   2 | 3 | 9

               6 | 11 | 5

Note.—This int. was unpaid and has been added to advances per Capital Discharge II., 2.

5. *On £50 4% Victory Bond—*

1931.

Sept. 1. ½ yr's int. to date £2 less tax at 4s. 6d., 9s. .   .   . £1 | 11 | 0

Less accrued int. included in price from 1st March to 10th July 1931 (131 days) 14s. 4d. less tax at 5s., 3s. 7d. .   .   .   0 | 10 | 9

            1 | 0 | 3

Note.—The rate of tax for 1931-2 was retrospectively increased to 5s. per £ in September 1931 as from 5th April 1931.

                                       204 | 12 | 2

SUM OF INCOME CHARGE .   .   .   .   £222 | 19 | 8

INCOME DISCHARGE

I. PAYMENTS TO LIFERENTRIX—Mrs Murray—

1931.

Feb. 28. Per Bank of Scotland, Edinburgh	£35	0	0
May 31. Do. Do. . . .	35	0	0
Aug. 31. Do. Do. . . .	35	0	0
Nov. 30. Do. Do. . . .	35	0	0

                                           £140 | 0 | 0

II. MANAGEMENT :—

1931.

Dec. 31. Thomas Murray, W.S., commission for year to date . . . . . . £7 | 10 | 0

Thomas Murray, W.S., posts, etc. .   .   0 | 2 | 6

                                           7 | 12 | 6

III. BALANCE OF INCOME at credit with Agent as at close of account   75 | 7 | 2

SUM OF INCOME DISCHARGE Equal to CHARGE   .   £222 | 19 | 8

CHAPTER XI

SPECIMEN TRUST ACCOUNTS SHOWING APPORTIONMENTS

Index and Summary of Apportionments in Specimen Accounts

1. *At Testator's Death.*—Preference stock held at date of testator's death is sold after receipt of an interim dividend, which is transferred to capital, in order to avoid two calculations, and added to the price realised. The apportionment is completed under No. 3.

2. *At Testator's Death.*—Preference stock is held at date of testator's death and the accrued dividend applicable to capital is calculated from the close of the previous year of the company until date of death.

3. *On Sale.*—This is the continuation of apportionment No. 1. The accrued dividend from date of death until date of sale is applicable to income, and deducted from the price realised.

4. *On Sale.*—Preference stock is sold during a company's year before any interim dividend is received. The amount of accrued dividend included in the price is calculated from the close of the previous year of the company until date of sale.

5. *On Sale.*—Ordinary stock held at date of testator's death is sold before any dividend is received. The accrued dividend included in the price was anticipated to be at 10% per annum, and is calculated from date of death until date of sale.

6. *At Testator's Death.*—Ordinary stock is held at date of testator's death. An interim dividend has been received prior to death, and the final dividend is apportioned, so that the sum remaining as applicable to income is the equivalent of the accrued dividend calculated at the *total annual rate* from date of death until the close of the company's year.

7. *On Sale.*—Ordinary stock is sold during a company's year before any interim dividend is received. The amount of accrued dividend is calculated at the anticipated annual rate of 10% from the close of the previous year of the company until date of sale.

8. *On Sale.*—Ordinary stock is sold during a company's year after receipt of an interim dividend. The amount of accrued dividend is calculated at the anticipated annual rate of 10% from the close of the previous year of the company until date of sale (8*a*), less the amount of interim dividend received (8*b*).

9. *On Sale.*—This is similar to No. 8 except that the sale is made after the close of the company's year, but before the receipt of the final

dividend, thus leaving accrued dividend for a period greater than a year (9*a*), subject to deduction of interim dividend received (9*b*).

10. *On Sale.*—Ordinary stock is sold as in No. 9, but the rate of final dividend has been declared prior to sale, although this dividend passes to the purchaser. The accrued dividend is, therefore, taken in two parts, (1) the final dividend completing the previous year of the company, (2) the anticipated dividend from the close of that year until date of sale.

11. *On Sale.*—Ordinary stock is sold as in No. 5. In this case the rate of dividend anticipated at date of sale is 6%, but only 5% is actually paid. The latter rate must be ignored in the account, although declared before the account is prepared.

12. *At Testator's Death.*—Ordinary stock is held at date of testator's death, on which no interim dividend has been received for the current year prior to death. The dividends received are added together and apportioned, so that the sum applicable to capital is the accrued dividend at the total annual rate from the close of the company's previous year until date of death.

13. *At Testator's Death.*—This is similar to No. 12 except that the first dividend received is declared as in respect of a half year and, accordingly, is apportioned without reference to any other dividend.

14. *On Purchase.*—Debenture stock (on which interest is declared half yearly) is purchased, and the first interest is apportioned so that the interest accrued from close of the previous half year until date of purchase is applicable to capital.

15. *On Purchase.*—Participating preference stock is purchased after an interim dividend has been paid for the current year. The final dividend is apportioned so that the sum remaining as applicable to income is the equivalent of the accrued dividend (calculated at the total annual rate) from date of purchase until the close of the company's year.

16. *On Purchase.*—Preference stock is purchased after the close of the company's year, but before the final dividend is paid. The dividends which are received are added together and apportioned so that the sum applicable to capital is the total accrued dividend from the close of the *previous* year of the company until the date of the purchase, *less* the interim dividend paid prior to purchase.

17. *On Purchase.*—5% Consolidated Loan (a fictitious British Government Security) is purchased after the stock is marked " ex dividend," but before the interest is due. No interest is receivable on this stock until 1st December (6½ months later). An apportionment is made so that accrued interest from date of purchase (15th May) until date of next interest (1st June) is *added* to the purchase price and credited to income.

18. *On Purchase.*—Further 5% Consolidated Loan is purchased. The accrued interest applicable to capital is calculated from the last date of payment of interest (1st June) until date of purchase (15th August).

19. *On Sale.*—Part of the Consolidated Loan holding is sold after the stock is marked " ex dividend," but before the interest is due, so that interest is received in respect of the period of 16 days after the stock is sold. When the interest is received an apportionment is made, so that the accrued interest for the period from date of sale to date of payment is taken as applicable to capital and, therefore, deducted from income.

20. *On Cessation of Liferent.*—Ordinary stock is held on which no interim dividend has been received for the current year. The accrued dividend applicable to period of the liferent is calculated from the close of the previous year of the company, at the rate anticipated at the time.

21. *On Cessation of Liferent.*—Ordinary stock is held on which two interim dividends have been received for the current year. The calculation is similar to No. 20 except that the interim dividends are deducted from the total sum accrued.

22. *On Cessation of Liferent.*—Debenture stock is held at close of the liferent. The accrued interest is calculated from the close of the previous half year.

23. *On Cessation of Liferent.*—Participating preference stock is held on which an interim dividend has been received. The calculation is similar to No. 21.

24. *On Cessation of Liferent.*—Preference stock is held on which an interim dividend has been received similarly to No. 23.

25. *On Cessation of Liferent.*—5% Consolidated Loan is held at the close of the liferent. The accrued interest is calculated as in No. 22.

26. *On Cessation of Liferent.*—A deposit receipt is held on which the accrued interest is ascertained by enquiry from the bank. Tax on this item is apportioned per Discharge, Branch I.

Note.—Examples of dividends " in bonis " are given as follows :

(1) At commencement of liferent—Income Charge I 6 (A/c of 1938-9).
(2) At cessation of liferent—Income Charge I 3 (A/c of 1940-1).

ACCOUNT CHARGE AND DISCHARGE of the Intromissions of Messrs Thomson & Co., Writers, as Agents for the Trustees of the late J. JONES.

From 31st March 1938 (date of testator's death)

To 31st December 1939.

Notes—(1). All purchases and sales shown on settlement dates, except where they are for cash settlement when the date of the contract is taken.

(2). Income tax assumed to be at 4s. per £ throughout.

CAPITAL CHARGE

I. ESTATE AS AT DATE OF DEATH :—

	£	s.	d.
1. £30,000 5% preference stock XY Co., Ltd.	£27,000	0	0
2. £50,000 ordinary stock XY Co., Ltd.	70,000	0	0
3. £10,000 Do. AB Co., Ltd.	11,000	0	0
4. £10,000 Do. CD Co., Ltd.	12,000	0	0
5. £10,000 Do. EF Co., Ltd.	13,000	0	0
6. £10,000 Do. GH Co., Ltd.	14,000	0	0
7. Furniture and personal effects	650	0	0
8. Sum at credit with Clydesdale Bank (current account)	1,500	0	0
	£149,150	0	0

II. ESTATE REALISED :—

1. XY Co., Ltd.—

(a) *Preference Stock.*

	Increase.			£	s.	d.
1938. June 30. Received proceeds of £20,000 5% pref. stock at 90% net after deduction of brokerage				£18,000	0	0
(1.) *Add* First half of div. for year to 30th Nov. 1938 received 31st May 1938 £500 less tax £100 (part of dividend of £600)				400	0	0
				£18,400	0	0
(3.) *Less* amount of dividend applicable to income from 31st March (date of death) to 30th June 1938 (date of sale) (91 days) £249, 6s. 4d. less tax £49, 17s. 4d.				199	9	0
Forward			£149,150	£18,200	11	0

CAPITAL CHARGE—(Continued).

II. ESTATE REALISED—(continued).
   1. XY Co., Ltd.—(continued).
     (a) Preference Stock—(continued).

		Forward	£ s. d.	£ s. d.	Increase. £ s. d.	Forward £149,150 0 0
(4.)	1938. Dec. 30. Received proceeds of £10,000 5% pref. stock at 90% net after deduction of brokerage		£9000 0 0	£18,200 11 0		
	Less amount of div. applicable to income from 30th Nov. to 30th Dec. 1938 (30 days) £41, 1s. 11d. less tax £8, 4s. 5d.		32 17 6			
			£8967 2 6			
(2.)	*Add* amount of dividend on £10,000 stock from 30th Nov. 1937 to 31st March 1938 (121 days) £165, 15s. 1d. less tax £33, 3s.		132 12 1	9,099 14 7		
				£27,300 5 7	£300 5 7	
	Note.					
	Cost per Branch I., No. 1		£27,000 0 0			
	Amount Received		27,300 5 7			
	Increase		£300 5 7			
	(b) *Ordinary Stock.*					
(5.)	1938. June 30. Received proceeds of £10,000 ord. stock at 150% net after deduction of brokerage		£15,000 0 0			
	Less amount of dividend at 10% per annum applicable to income from 31st March to 30th June 1938 (91 days) £249, 6s. 4d. less tax £49, 17s. 3d.		199 9 1			
			£14,800 10 11			
	1938. Aug. 31. Received proceeds of £10,000 ord. stock at 160% x.d. net after deduction of brokerage	£16,000 0 0				

Ref.	Description		£	s	d	£	s	d	£	s	d	£	s	d	£	s	d
												0	0				
												£149,150	0	0			
												£300	5	7			
												£27,300	5	7			
(7.)	*Less* amount of div. at 10% per annum applicable to income from 31st May to 31st Aug. 1938 (92 days) £252, 1s. 1d. less tax £50, 8s. 3d.	201	12	10	15,798	7	2										
(6.)	1938. Sept. 1. Proportion of final div. for year to 31st May 1938 representing period prior to 31st March 1938, per Income Ch. I, 2				1,705	4	2										
(8b.)	1939. Apr. 30. Received proceeds of £10,000 ord. stock at 155% net after deduction of brokerage	£15,500	0	0													
	Add Interim div. of 3% for year to 31st May 1939 £300 less tax £60	240	0	0													
		£15,740	0	0													
		732	1	1													
(8a.)	*Less* amount of div. at 10% per annum applicable to income from 31st May 1938 to 30th April 1939 (334 days) £915, 1s. 4d., less tax £183, 0s. 3d.				15,007	18	11										
(9b.)	1939. June 30. Received proceeds of £10,000 ord. stock at 140% net after deduction of brokerage	£14,000	0	0													
	Add Interim div. of 3% for year to 31st May 1939 £300 less tax £60	240	0	0													
		£14,240	0	0													
		865	15	1													
(9a.)	*Less* amount of div. at 10% per annum applicable to income from 31st May 1938 to 30th June 1939 (1 year and 30 days) £1082, 3s. 10d. less tax £216, 8s. 9d.				13,374	4	11										
	Forward				£60,686	6	1										

G

CAPITAL CHARGE—(Continued)

II. ESTATE REALISED—(continued).
1. XY Co. Ltd.—(continued).

(b) Ordinary Stock—(continued.)

		Forward	£60,686	6	1	£27,300	5	7	£149,150	0	0

(10.) 1939. Aug. 20. Received proceeds of £10,000 ord. stock at 150% c.d. net after deduction of brokerage . . . £15,000 0 0

Less amount of div. applicable to income:—

	£	s.	d.			
(1) Final div. for year to 31st May 1939 of 7% £700 less tax £140 .	£560	0	0			
(2) Div. at 10% per annum from 31st May to 20th Aug. 1939 (81 days) £221, 18s. 4d. less tax £44, 7s. 8d. .	177	10	8			
	737	10	8			

			14,262	9	4						
			£74,948	15	0						
			70,000	0	0						

Increase . . . . . £4,948 15 5 . . 74,948 15 5 . . 4,948 15 5

Note.—Cost per Br. I, No. 2

2. AB Co., Ltd.—

(11.) 1938. Apr. 30. Received proceeds of £10,000 ord. stock at 120% net after deduction of brokerage . . . £12,000 0 0

Less amount of div. at 6% per annum applicable to income from 31st March to 30th April 1938 (30 days) £49, 6s. 3d. less tax £9, 17s. 3d. . . . 39 9 0

	£11,960	11	0	11,960	11	0
	11,000	0	0			

Note.—Cost per Br. I, No. 3

4. *5% Consolidated Loan* :—

1939. Nov. 15. Received proceeds of £1000 stock at 101% x.d. net after deduction of brokerage . . . £1,010 0 0

(19.) *Add* accrued interest from 15th Nov. to 1st Dec. 1939 (16 days) due by income £2, 3s. 10d. less tax 8s. 9d. . 1 15 1

1,011 15 1

5. *Add* amount of accrued income, as detailed below . 543 13 3

£6,209 12 0

6,209 12 0

£117,265 0 4

£155,359 12 0

Note of Accrued Income as at 31st March 1938 :—

	Value as at Date of Death.	Less Accrued Income.	Net Amount of Capital.
(12.) CD Co., Ltd., £10,000 ordinary stock	£12,000 0 0	£265 4 2	£11,734 15 10
(13.) EF Co., Ltd., £10,000 Do.	13,000 0 0	278 9 1	12,721 10 11
	£25,000 0 0	£543 13 3	£24,456 6 9

SUM OF THE CAPITAL CHARGE

CAPITAL DISCHARGE

I. DEATHBED AND FUNERAL EXPENSES :—

1938. Apr. 30. Dr Merrilees' fee for professional services . £105 0 0

Burke & Co., undertakers for funeral . 95 0 0

Aug. 1. Bruce Brothers for tombstone . 150 0 0

£350 0 0

II. DEBTS DUE BY DECEASED :—

1938. July 1. Mrs Jones for household accounts and wages £250 0 0

Bank of Scotland repayment of overdraft 1050 0 0

1,300 0 0

Forward £1,650 0 0

CAPITAL DISCHARGE—(Continued)

				£	s	d
			Forward	£1,650	0	0
III. GOVERNMENT DUTY :—						
1938. May 31. Estate Duty 22% on £147,500 (being net estate after deduction of funeral expenses and debts)				32,450	0	0
Note.—Legacy duty on the liferent has been paid by the liferenter.						
IV. LEGAL AND MISCELLANEOUS EXPENSES :—						
1939. Dec. 31. Agents' Business Account and Outlays including commission on cash transactions				1,500	0	0
V. INVESTMENTS MADE :—						
1. *XX Ltd.*—						
1938. Sept. 30. Cost of £20,000 5% debenture stock at 90% including stamp and brokerage		£18,000 0 0				
(14.) *Less* amount of interest included in purchase price from 30th June to 30th Sept. 1938 (92 days)		201 12 10				
£252, 1s. 1d. less tax £50, 8s. 3d.				£17,798	7	2
2. *YY Ltd.*—						
1939. Apr. 30. Cost of £15,000 5% participating preference stock at 105% including stamp and brokerage		£15,750 0 0				
(15.) *Less* amount of dividend included in purchase price, per Income Charge I, 8		523 11 2				
				15,226	8	10
3. *WW Ltd.*—						
1939. June 30. Cost of £20,000 5% preference stock at 85% including stamp and brokerage		£17,000 0 0				
Less amount of dividend at 5% per annum included in purchase price from 31st May 1938 to 30th June 1939 (1 year and 30 days)	£865 15 1					
£1082, 3s. 10d. less tax £216, 8s. 9d.						
Less dividend paid prior to purchase £500 less tax £100	400 0 0					
(16.)		465 15 1				
				16,534	4	11
4. *5% Consolidated Loan*—						
1939. May 15. Cost of £1000 stock at 101% x.d. including stamp and brokerage		£1,010 0 0				
(17.) *Add* accrued interest from 15th May to 1st June 1939 (17 days) due to income		1 17 3				
£2, 6s. 7d. less tax 9s. 4d.		£1,011 17 3				

1939. Aug. 15. Cost of £15,000 stock at 102% including stamp and brokerage £15,300 0 0

(18.) Less amount of interest included in purchase price from 1st June to 15th Aug. 1939 (75 days) £154, 2s. 2d. less tax £30, 16s. 5d. . . 123 5 9

		15,176	14	3	
					16,188 11 6

Note.—Cost of £16,000 stock as above £16,188 11 6
Less proceeds of £1000 stock, per Charge Br. II., 4 . . 1,011 15 1

Cost of £15,000 stock per Funds at close of account . . £15,176 16 5 . . . £65,747 12 5

VI. DEPOSIT RECEIPT:—
1939. Sept. 1. Placed on Deposit Receipt with Bank of Scotland . . £15,000 0 0

VII. ESTATE AS AT CLOSE OF THIS ACCOUNT AT COST:—

1. £10,000 ordinary stock CD Co., Ltd. . . . £11,734 15 10
2. £10,000 ordinary stock EF Co., Ltd. . . . 12,721 10 11
3. £10,000 ordinary stock GH Co., Ltd. . . . 14,000 0 0
4. £20,000 5% debenture stock XX Ltd. . . . 17,798 7 2
5. £15,000 5% participating preference stock YY Ltd. . 15,226 8 10
6. £20,000 5% preference stock WW Ltd. . . . 16,534 4 11
7. £15,000 5% Consolidated Loan 15,176 16 5
8. Furniture and personal effects 650 0 0

£103,842 4 1

Add Sum on Deposit Receipt with Bank of Scotland dated 1st September 1939 . . 15,000 0 0
Capital Balance uninvested 917 7 11

119,759 12 0

SUM OF CAPITAL DISCHARGE equal to CHARGE £155,359 12 0

G 2

INCOME CHARGE

I. DIVIDENDS AND INTEREST RECEIVED :—

	Detail	£	s	d	£	s	d
	1. On £30,000 5% Preference Stock XY Co., Ltd.—						
	1938. May 31. First half of div. for year to 30th Nov. 1938 on £30,000 stock £750 less tax £150				£600	0	0
	Less transferred to capital in respect of :—						
(1.)	(1) Whole div. on £20,000 stock sold 30th June 1938 £500 less tax £100	£400	0	0			
(2.)	(2) Amount of dividend at 5% per annum on remaining £10,000 stock from 30th Nov. 1937 to 31st March 1938 (121 days) £165, 15s. 1d. less tax £33, 3s.	132	12	1	532	12	1
	Balance representing net dividend on £10,000 stock (part retained) from 31st March to 31st May 1938				£67	7	11
(3.)	1938. June 30. Accrued div. on £20,000 stock from 31st March to 30th June 1938 (date of sale) (91 days) £249, 6s. 4d. less tax £49, 17s. 4d.				199	9	0
	Nov. 30. Second ½ yr's div. on account of year to date on £10,000 stock £250, less tax £50				200	0	0
(4.)	Dec. 30. Accrued div. on £10,000 stock from 30th Nov. to 30th Dec. 1938 (date of sale) (30 days) £41, 1s. 11d. less tax £8, 4s. 5d.				32	17	6
					£499	14	5
	2. On £50,000 Ordinary Stock XY Co., Ltd.—						
(5.)	1938. June 30. Accrued div. on £10,000 stock at 10% per annum from 31st March to 30th June 1938 (date of sale) (91 days) £249, 6s. 4d. less tax £49, 17s. 3d.				£199	9	1
	Sept. 1. Final div. for year to 31st May 1938 on £40,000 stock at 7% (making 10% with the interim div. received by testator) £2800 less tax £560	£2240	0	0			
(6.)	*Less transferred to capital (being the difference to bring out the undernoted balance)*	1705	4	2			
	Balance representing accrued div. at 10% per annum from 31st March to 31st May 1938 (61 days) on £40,000 stock £668, 9s. 10d. less tax £133, 14s.				534	15	10
(7.)	1938. Aug. 31. Accrued div. on £10,000 stock at 10% per annum from 31st May to 31st Aug. 1938 (date of sale) (92 days) £252, 1s. 1d. less tax £50, 8s. 3d.				201	12	10
	1939. Feb. 28. Interim div. for year to 31st May 1939 on £30,000 stock at 3% £900 less tax £180				720	0	0
(8a.)	Apr. 30. Accrued div. on £10,000 stock at 10% per annum from 31st May 1938 to 30th Apr. 1939 (date of sale) (334 days) £915, 1s. 4d. less tax £183, 0s. 3d.	£732	1	1			
(8b.)	*Less interim div. of 3% included above (part of £720) on 28th Feb. 1939 £300 less tax £60*	240	0	0			

		£	s.	d.	£	s.	d.	£	s.	d.
								3,511	4	7
(9a.)	1939. June 30. Accrued div. on £10,000 stock at 10% per annum from 31st May 1938 to 30th June 1939 (date of sale) (1 year and 30 days) £1082, 3s. 10d. less tax £216, 8s. 9d.	£865	15	1						
(9b.)	Less interim div. of 3% included above on 28th Feb. 1939 (part of £720) £300 less tax £60	240	0	0						
(9.)					625	15	1			
(10.)	1939. Aug. 20. Accrued div. on £10,000 stock sold this date :—									
	(a) Final div. of 7% for year to 31st May 1939 £700 less tax £140	£560	0	0						
	(b) Div. at 10% per annum from 31st May to 20th Aug. 1939 (date of sale) (81 days) £221, 18s. 4d. less tax £44, 7s. 8d.	177	10	8						
					737	10	8			
	Notes—(1). On 1st Sept. 1939 a final dividend of 7% was received on £10,000 stock = £700 less £140, £560, but this stock had been sold cum. dividend and this sum was therefore paid over to the purchaser.									
	(2). The anticipated rate of div. was 10% at the time of each sale and in fact this was the actual rate.									
(11.)	3. *On £10,000 Ordinary Stock AB Co., Ltd.*—									
	1938. Apr. 30. Accrued div. at 6% per annum from 31st March to 30th April 1938 (date of sale) (30 days) £49, 6s. 3d. less tax £9, 17s. 3d.							39	9	0
	Notes—(1). No dividends received by Trustees during period prior to sale.									
	(2). At the time of sale 6% was the anticipated rate for the year, but the rate actually paid was 5% and this was known before the account was prepared, but must not be considered.									
(12.)	4. *On £10,000 Ordinary Stock CD Co., Ltd.*—									
	1938. May 28. Interim div. of 5% for year to 30th Nov. 1938 £500 less tax £100	£400	0	0						
	1939. Jan. 31. Final Do.	400	0	0						
					£800	0	0			
	Less Proportion thereof applicable to capital at 10% per annum from 30th Nov. 1937 to 31st March 1938 (121 days) £331, 10s. 2d. less tax £66, 6s.				265	4	2			
								534	15	10
	Forward							£4,585	3	10

INCOME CHARGE—(Continued)

I. DIVIDENDS AND INTEREST RECEIVED—(continued)

	£	s.	d.	£	s.	d.
Forward				4,585	3	10

5. On £10,000 Ordinary Stock EF Co., Ltd.—

(13.)

1938. July 31. Div. of 7% for half-year to 30th June 1938 (181 days) £700 less tax £140 . . . £560 0 0

Less Proportion thereof applicable to capital from 31st Dec. 1937 to 31st March 1938 (90 days) 90/181 × £700 = £348, 1s. 4d. less tax £69, 12s. 3d. . . . 278 9 1

£281 10 11

1939. Apr. 30. Div. of 3% on account of year to 30th June 1939 £300 less tax £60 . . . 240 0 0 . . . 521 10 11

Note.—No further dividends were received for year 1938-39.

6. On £10,000 Ordinary Stock GH Co., Ltd.—

1938. Aug. 31. Final div. of 3% for year to 31st July 1938 £300 less tax £60 . . . £240 0 0

Note.—The interim div. of 7% was paid on 28th Feb. 1938 (prior to the death of the testator). The proportion of income which should have been applicable to income from 31st March to 31st July 1938 at 10% per annum (122 days) is £334, 4s. 11d. less tax £66, 17s.=£267, 7s. 11d. No further sum can be apportioned as it is against the legal principles of apportionment to take from capital any part of the estate at date of death.

1939. Feb. 28. Interim div. of 3% for year to 31st July 1939 £300 less tax £60 . . . 240 0 0

Aug. 31. Final Do. . . . 240 0 0

Nov. 30. Interim div. of 3% for year to 31st July 1940 £300 less tax £60 . . . 240 0 0 . . . 960 0 0

7. On £20,000 5% Deb. Stock XX, Ltd.—

(14.)

1938. Dec. 31. ½ yr's int. to date £500 less tax £100 . . . £400 0 0

Less interest included in purchase price from 30th June to 30th September 1938 (92 days) £252, 1s. 1d., less tax £50, 8s. 3d. . . . 201 12 10

£198 7 2

1939. June 30. ½ yr's int. to date £500 less tax £100 . . . Do. . . . 400 0 0

Dec. 31. Do. Do. . . . 400 0 0 . . . 998 7 2

	Particulars	£ s. d.	£ s. d.	£ s. d.
8.	On £15,000 5% *Participating Preference Stock YY, Ltd.*—			
	1939. July 31. Final div. of 5% (making 7½%), for year to 31st May 1939 £750 less tax £150 .		£600 0 0	
(15.)	*Less* dividend included in purchase price, being the difference to bring out the undernoted balance .		523 11 2	
	Balance representing accrued div. at 7½% from 30th April to 31st May 1939 (31 days) £95, 11s. less tax £19, 2s. 2d. .		£76 8 10	
	1939. Dec. 15. Interim div. of 2½% for year to 31st May 1940 £375 less tax £75 .		300 0 0	
				376 8 10
9.	On £20,000 5% *Preference Stock WW, Ltd.*—			
	1939. July 31. Final ½ yr's div. on account of year to 31st May 1939 £500 less tax £100 .		£400 0 0	
	Dec. 31. First ½ yr's div. on account of year to 31st May 1940 £500 less tax £100 .		400 0 0	
			£800 0 0	
(16.)	*Less* div. included in purchase price at 5% per annum from 31st May 1938 to 30th June 1939 (1 year and 30 days) £1082, 3s. 10d. less tax £216, 8s. 9d. .	£865 15 1		
	Less div. paid prior to purchase £500 less tax £100 (being the first half year's div. on account of year to 31st May 1939) .	400 0 0	465 15 1	
				334 4 11
10.	On £1000, *afterwards* £16,000, *now* £15,000 5% *Consolidated Loan*—			
	1939. May 15. Accrued int. on £1000 stock from 15th May to 1st June 1939 (17 days) £2, 6s. 7d. less tax 9s. 4d. .		£1 17 3	
(17.)				
	Dec. 1. ½ yr's int. to date on £16,000 stock (no tax deducted) .	£400 0 0		
(18.)	*Less* int. included in purchase price of £15,000 stock from 1st June to 15th Aug. 1939 (75 days) £154, 2s. 2d. less tax £30, 16s. 5d. .	123 5 9		
		£276 14 3		
(19.)	*Less* int. accrued on £1000 stock from 15th Nov. (date of sale) to 1st Dec. 1939 (16 days) £2, 3s. 10d. less tax 8s. 9d. .	1 15 1	274 19 2	
				276 16 5
	SUM OF THE INCOME CHARGE .			£8,052 12 1

INCOME DISCHARGE

I. INCOME TAX :—
Sum reserved at 4s. per £ on £400 Consolidated Loan interest received 1st December 1939　.　　£80 0 0
Note.—Apportionment between capital and income has been made by taking all items net.

II. INTEREST :—
1938. May 31.　Interest on Government Duty at 4% from date of death on £32,450　.　£216 18 6
　　　Dec. 31.　Bank overdraft interest to date in respect of temporary advances to pay duties　.　151 2 0　|　368 0 6

III. ANNUITY :—
1939. Mar. 31.　Miss Jemima Jones—annuity for year to date £100 less tax £20　.　　80 0 0

IV. MANAGEMENT :—
1939. Dec. 31.　Agents' commission for collection of income and preparation of this account　.　450 0 0

V. FREE INCOME for period transferred to the Liferenter's personal account appended　.　7,074 11 7
Author's Notes.—(1). This is a balancing figure to square off the account.
　　　(2). Personal account not detailed, but should form an appendix showing receipts and payments for period.

SUM OF INCOME DISCHARGE equal to CHARGE　.　　£8,052 12 1

Example of Account in a Trust at close of Liferent to show Apportionments.

ACCOUNT CHARGE AND DISCHARGE of the Intromissions
of Messrs Thomson & Co., Writers, as Agents for the Trustees
of the late J. JONES.

From 31st December 1939
To 31st December 1941.

Notes—(1). The liferenter died on 31st January 1941.
(2). Income tax assumed to be at 4s. per £ throughout.

CAPITAL CHARGE

ESTATE AS AT CLOSE OF LAST ACCOUNT AT COST :—			
1. £10,000 ordinary stock CD Co., Ltd.	£11,734	15	10
2. £10,000 ordinary stock EF Co., Ltd.	12,721	10	11
3. £10,000 ordinary stock GH Co., Ltd.	14,000	0	0
4. £20,000 5% debenture stock XX Ltd.	17,798	7	2
5. £15,000 5% participating preference stock YY Ltd. . . .	15,226	8	10
6. £20,000 5% preference stock WW Ltd.	16,534	4	11
7. £15,000 5% Consolidated Loan	15,176	16	5
8. Furniture and personal effects	650	0	0
	£103,842	4	1
Add Sum on Deposit Receipt with Bank of Scotland dated 1st Sept. 1939	15,000	0	0
Capital Balance uninvested	917	7	11
	£119,759	12	0

ESTATE REALISED :—
1941. Mar. 1. Received proceeds of £15,000 5% Consolidated Loan at 102% net after deduction of brokerage . . . . £15,300 | 0 | 0
Note.—Cost per Branch I., 7 . . . . 15,176 | 16 | 5

Increase	123	3	7

Note.—No distinction need now be made between Capital and Income so no apportionment is required.

INCREASE ON REVALUATION OF ESTATE per Discharge V. . .	334	12	4
FREE INCOME RECEIVED AFTER CESSATION OF LIFERENT per Income Discharge V. transferred for division with residue of estate . . .	5,049	15	1

DEPOSIT RECEIPT UPLIFTED :—
1941. Mar. 1. Deposit Receipt p. £15,000 with Bank of Scotland dated 1st Sept. 1939 . . . . £15,000 0 0

SUM OF CAPITAL CHARGE	£125,267	3	0

CAPITAL DISCHARGE

GOVERNMENT DUTIES :—			
1941. Mar. 1. Estate Duty 22% on amount of estate at date of liferenter's death £120,000	£26,400	0	0
Legacy duty on residue 5% on £93,600 . . .	4,680	0	0
Forward	£31,080	0	0

CAPITAL DISCHARGE—(*Continued*)   Forward | £31,080 | 0

II. ADVANCES TO BENEFICIARIES :—
1941. Dec. 15. Thomas Jones on account of share

of residue	£1000	0	0
James Wilson on account of share of residue	500	0	0
	£1500	0	0

III. AMOUNT OF ACCRUED INCOME AS AT 31ST JANUARY 1941 (the date of death of the liferenter) . . . .   1,551 | 15

Note.—This sum has been transferred to Income Charge, as follows :—

£10,000 ordinary stock CD Co., Ltd. . . .	£471	4	8
£10,000 ordinary stock EF Co., Ltd. . . .	71	4	8
£20,000 5% deb. stock XX Ltd.	67	18	11
£15,000 5% participating pref. stock YY Ltd. .	304	2	2
£20,000 5% pref. stock WW Ltd. . . .	136	19	9
£15,000 5% Consolidated Loan	100	5	6
Deposit Receipt p. £15,000	400	0	0
	£1551	15	8

IV. MANAGEMENT :—
1941. Dec. 31. Agents' business account and commission on cash transactions to date including winding up

trust	£325	0	0
Agents' outlays	10	0	0

                                                                    335 | 0

V. ESTATE AS AT CLOSE OF THIS ACCOUNT AS REVALUED FOR DIVISION :—

	Note of Cost.			Present Revaluation.		
1. £10,000 ord. stock CD Co., Ltd.	£11,734	15	10	£11,500	0	0
2. £10,000 ord. stock EF Co., Ltd.	12,721	10	11	12,750	0	0
3. £10,000 ord. stock GH Co., Ltd.	14,000	0	0	14,200	0	0
4. £20,000 5% deb. stock XX Ltd.	17,798	7	2	18,000	0	0
5. £15,000 5% participating pref. stock YY Ltd. . . .	15,226	8	10	15,150	0	0
6. £20,000 5% pref. stock WW Ltd.	16,534	4	11	16,750	0	0
7. Furniture and personal effects .	650	0	0	650	0	0
8. Advance to T. Jones on account of Residue	1,000	0	0	1,000	0	0
9. Advance to J. Wilson on account of Residue	500	0	0	500	0	0
	£90,165	7	8	£90,500	0	0
Add Balance at credit with Agents	1,800	7	4	1,800	7	4
	£91,965	15	0	£92,300	7	4

                                                               92,300 | 7

91,965	15	0

Increase transferred to Charge III. . . . | £334 | 12 | 4

SUM OF CAPITAL DISCHARGE equal to CHARGE . . . . | £125,267 | 3

INCOME CHARGE

DIVIDENDS AND INTEREST APPLICABLE TO PERIOD FROM 31ST DECEMBER 1939 TO 31ST JANUARY 1941 (DATE OF DEATH OF THE LIFERENTER) :—

1. *On £10,000 Ord. Stock CD Co., Ltd.*—

		£	s	d	£	s	d
1940. Feb. 28. Interim div. of 5% for year to 30th June 1940 £500 less tax £100		400	0	0			
July 31. Final Do. Do.		400	0	0			
1941. Jan. 31. Div. accrued to date at 10% per annum from 30th June 1940 (215 days) £589, 0s. 10d. less tax £117, 16s. 2d. .		471	4	8			
Note.—10% was the anticipated rate at that date.							
					£1,271	4	8

2. *On £10,000 Ord. Stock EF Co., Ltd.*—

	£	s	d	£	s	d
1940. Jan. 1. Quarter's div. of 2% on account of year to 30th June 1940 £200 less tax £40 . .	£160	0	0			
Apr. 1. Quarter's div. of 2½% on account of year to 30th June 1940 £250 less tax £50 . .	200	0	0			
July 1. Final div. of 2½% (making 7%) for year to 30th June 1940 £250 less tax £50 . .	200	0	0			
Oct. 1. First quarter's div. of 2½% on account of year to 30th June 1941 £250 less tax £50 .	200	0	0			
1941. Jan. 1. Second Do. Do.	200	0	0			
Jan. 31. Div. accrued to date at 10% per annum from 30th June 1940 (215 days) £589, 0s. 10d. less tax £117, 16s. 2d. £471 4 8						
Less two interim dividends already received £500 less tax £100 . 400 0 0						
	71	4	8			
				1,031	4	8

Note.—10% was the anticipated rate at that date.

3. *On £10,000 Ord. Stock GH Co., Ltd.*—

	£	s	d	£	s	d
1940. Aug. 31. Final div. of 3% for year to 31st July 1940 £300 less tax £60	£240	0	0			
Dec. 31. Interim div. of 3% and special bonus of 2% for year to 31st July 1941 £500 less tax £100	400	0	0			
				640	0	0

Note.—No further apportionment can be made as the position is similar to that arising at commencement of a Trust where the testator has received a larger share of income than would be due if apportioned.

	£	s	d
The amount of income at 8% per annum which should have been applicable to income for period from 31st July 1940 to 31st January 1941 (184 days) £403, 5s. 9d. less tax £80, 13s. 2d. .	£322	12	7
Sum actually received	400	0	0
Excess	£77	7	5

8% was the anticipated rate for the year at that date, as the final dividend was expected to be 3%. It was actually 4%.

	£	s	d
Forward	£2,942	9	4

INCOME CHARGE—(*Continued*)   Forward ‖ £2,942 | 9

I. DIVIDENDS AND INTEREST, ETC.—(*continued*)

4. *On £20,000 5% Deb. Stock XX Ltd.—*

1940. June 30.   ½ yr's int. to date £500 less tax
        £100   .   .   .   . ‖ £400 | 0 | 0
   Dec. 31.   Do.   Do.   400 | 0 | 0
(22.) 1941. Jan. 31. Interest accrued to date from 31st
        Dec. 1940 (31 days) £84, 18s. 8d. less tax
        £16, 19s. 9d.   .   .   .   .   .   . ‖ 67 | 18 | 11

                                                                867 | 18

5. *On £15,000 5% Participating Pref. Stock YY Ltd.—*

1940. July 31.   Final div. of 5% (making 7½%) for year
        to 31st May 1940 £750 less tax £150   .   . ‖ £600 | 0 | 0
   Dec. 15.   Interim div. of 2½% for year to 31st May
        1941 £375 less tax £75   .   .   .   . ‖ 300 | 0 | 0
(23.) 1941. Jan. 31.   Div. accrued to date (made up as
        below)   .   .   .   . ‖ 304 | 2 | 2
        7½% per annum from 31st May 1940
            to 31st Jan. 1941 (245 days)
            £755, 2s. 9d. less tax £151, 0s. 7d.   £604   2   2
        Less interim div. already received £375
        less tax £75   300   0   0
                                    ——————————
                                    £304   2   2
                                    ══════════

Note.—It was anticipated at that date that the final
        div. would be at 5%.

                                                               1,204 | 2

6. *On £20,000 5% Pref. Stock WW Ltd.—*

1940. June 30.   Final ½ yr's div. on account of year to
        31st May 1940 £500 less tax £100   .   . ‖ £400 | 0 | 0
   Dec. 31.   First ½ yr's div. on account of year to
        31st May 1941 £500 less tax £100   .   . ‖ 400 | 0 | 0
   1941. Jan. 31.   Div. accrued to date (made up as
        below)   .   .   .   . ‖ 136 | 19 | 9
(24.)   5% per annum from 31st May 1940
            to 31st Jan. 1941 (245 days)
            £671, 4s. 8d. less tax £134, 4s. 11d.   £536 19   9
        Less first ½ yr's div. already received
            £500 less tax £100 .   .   .   400   0   0
                                    ——————————
                                    £136 19   9
                                    ══════════

                                                                936 | 19

7. *On £15,000 5% Consolidated Loan—*

1940. June 1.   ½ yr's int. to date (no tax deducted)   . ‖ £375 | 0 | 0
   Dec. 1.   Do.   Do.   375 | 0 | 0
(25.) 1941. Jan. 31. Int. accrued to date from 1st Dec. 1940
        (61 days) £125, 6s. 10d. less tax £25, 1s. 4d.   . ‖ 100 | 5 | 6

                                                                850 | 5

8. *On Deposit Receipt—*

(26.) 1941. Jan. 31. Int. accrued to date on £15,000 from 1st Sept.
        1939, as certified by Bank of Scotland (no tax deducted)   . ‖ 400 | 0

                                          Forward ‖ £7,201 | 15

INCOME CHARGE—*(Continued)*			Forward	£7,201	15	8

DIVIDENDS AND INTEREST RECEIVED FROM 31ST JAN. 1941 TO 31ST DEC. 1941 :—

   Note.—No distinction is now necessary between Capital and Income as the liferent has ceased, so no apportionments are made. A proportion of the undernoted income is already included above on cessation of the liferent.

1. *On £10,000 Ord. Stock CD Co., Ltd.—*

1941. Feb. 28. Interim div. of 5% for year to 30th June 1941 £500 less tax £100 . . .		£400	0	0		
July 31. Final Do. Do.		400	0	0		
		£800	0	0		

2. *On £10,000 Ord. Stock EF Co., Ltd.—*

1941. Apr. 1. Third quarter's div. of 2½% on account of year to 30th June 1941 £250 less tax £50 . . .	£200	0	0			
July 1. Fourth Do.	200	0	0			
Oct. 1. First quarter's div. of 2½% on account of year to 30th June 1942 £250 less tax £50 . . .	200	0	0			
				600	0	0

3. *On £10,000 Ord. Stock GH Co., Ltd.—*

1941. Aug. 31. Final div. of 4% for year to 31st July 1941 £400 less tax £80 . . .				320	0	0

   Note.—In Branch I., 3, the estimate of this div. was 3% which at 31st Jan. 1941 was in accordance with the information available.

4. *On £20,000 5% Deb. Stock XX Ltd.—*

1941. June 30. ½ yr's int. to date £500 less tax £100	£400	0	0			
Dec. 31. Do.	400	0	0			
				800	0	0

5. *On £15,000 5% Participating Pref. Stock YY Ltd.—*

1941. July 31. Final div. of 5% (making 7½%) for year to 31st May 1941 £750 less tax £150 . . .	£600	0	0			
Dec. 15. Interim div. of 2½% for year to 31st May 1942 £375 less tax £75	300	0	0			
				900	0	0

6. *On £20,000 5% Pref. Stock WW Ltd.—*

1941. June 30. Final ½ yr's div. on account of year to 31st May 1941 £500 less tax £100 . . .	£400	0	0			
Dec. 31. First ½ yr's div. on account of year to 31st May 1942 £500 less tax £100	400	0	0			
				800	0	0

7. *On £15,000 5% Consolidated Loan—*

1941. June 1. ½ yr's int. to date (no tax deducted)	£375	0	0			
Dec. 1. Do.	375	0	0			
				750	0	0

	Forward	£4,970	0	0	£7,201	15	8

INCOME CHARGE—(*Continued*)   Forward   £7,201 | 15

II. DIVIDENDS AND INTEREST, ETC.—(*continued*) Forward	£4,970	0	0		
8. *On Advances to Beneficiaries at 5%—*					
1941. Dec. 31. Thos. Jones int. on £1000 from 15th inst. (16 days) £2, 3s. 10d. less tax 8s. 9d.	£1	15	1		
James Wilson int. on £500 from 15th inst. (16 days) £1, 1s. 11d. less tax 4s. 5d.	0	17	6		
		2	12	7	
9. *On Deposit Receipt—*					
1941. Mar. 1. On £15,000 dated 1st Sept. 1939 (no tax deducted)	450	0	0		
				5,422	12
SUM OF INCOME CHARGE				£12,624	8

INCOME DISCHARGE.

	Period from 31st December 1939 to 31st January 1941.			Period from 31st January 1941 to 31st December 19.	
I. INCOME TAX:—					
1940. May 1. Income Tax 1939-40 on £400 Consolidated Loan int. received 1st Dec. 1939 . .	£80	0	0		
Less reserved per last account	80	0	0		
Dec. 31. Income Tax 1940-41 on £750 Consolidated Loan int. received 1st June 1940 and 1st December 1940	£150	0	0		
1941. Dec. 31. Income Tax 1941-42 on Do. 1st June 1941 and 1st December 1941 . .				£150	0
Note.—Apportionment as at date of liferenter's death has been made by taking accrued int. net. Additional Income Tax 1940-41 on £450 Deposit Receipt int. received 1st March 1941 (whereof £400 accrued prior to 31st Jan. 1941) . .	80	0	0	10	0
	£230	0	0	£160	0

II. ANNUITY :—							
1940. Mar. 31. Miss Jemima Jones—annuity for year to date £100 less tax £20	£80	0	0				
1941. Mar. 31. Do.	80	0	0				
June 30. Do.—annuity to date of death (91 days) 91/365 × £100 = £24, 18s. 8d. less tax £4, 19s. 9d.	19	18	11				
	£179	18	11				
Whereof applicable to period of liferent from 31st March 1939 to 31st Jan. 1941 (1 year and 306 days) £183, 16s. 9d. less tax £36, 15s. 4d. . . .	147	1	5				
				147	1	5	32	17
Forward				£377	1	5	£192	17

INCOME DISCHARGE—(*Continued*)

	Period from 31st December 1939 to 31st January 1941.			Period from 31st January 1941 to 31st December 1941.		
Forward	£377	1	5	£192	17	6
MANAGEMENT :—						
1941. Jan. 31. Agents' commission for collection of income and preparation of this account to date	250	0	0			
Dec. 31. Do. Do.				180	0	0
FREE INCOME FOR PERIOD FROM 31ST DEC. 1939 TO 31ST JAN. 1941 :—						
Transferred to Liferenter's personal account in appendix (not shown)	6574	14	3			
Author's Note.—This is a balancing figure to square off this part of account.						
FREE INCOME FOR PERIOD FROM 31ST JAN. TO 31ST DEC. 1941 :—						
Available for division and transferred to Capital Account				5,049	15	1
	£7201	15	8	£5,422	12	7
				7,201	15	8
SUM OF INCOME DISCHARGE equal to CHARGE . . .				£12,624	8	3

H

CHAPTER XII

ESTATE DUTY

I. Introduction

ESTATE duty was first imposed by the Finance Act, 1894, but its scope and complications have been very much increased by subsequent Finance Acts. Numerous cases as to the interpretation of the law have received the attention of the courts, and some of the most important of these are noted in the following pages. (Sections of an Act are in Finance Act, 1894, unless otherwise stated.)

Liability to Duty.

Estate duty is primarily a duty on property (including investments, money and other assets) which passes to another person on the occasion of a death. In order to prevent evasion there is also liability on some other property which does not pass, but which is " deemed to pass " for duty purposes. The effect of Section 1 is that property passes if it has a continuous existence both before and after the death, and if it falls to a new owner on the death, such as investments and bank balances owned by deceased. Debts payable and deathbed and funeral expenses are allowable deductions. As explained below in more detail, under section 2 property passing is also deemed to include, for example, life policies maturing on the death, and property given away by the deceased shortly before his death. Under Finance Act, 1930, secs. 34 and 35, where property has been transferred to a company (whether by the absolute owner or by the liferenter and fiar), and income from it continues to be receivable, liability to estate duty may arise on the death of the former owner (or liferenter). In view of the complexity of the provisions as to companies no further reference is made to them owing to considerations of space.

Time of Property Passing.

For duty purposes, property passing on the death includes property passing immediately or after any interval, whether certainly or contingently, at a period ascertainable only by reference to the death (sec. 22, 1 (*l*)).

Settled Property.

Settled property is the name given to property held in trust under will, deed of trust, or other settlement, and, it has been said, " includes every device by which property may be enjoyed by different persons succeeding to the estate under the same deed." The settlor is the truster—*i.e.* he who places the property in trust.

Cesser of Interest.

The death of an annuitant or liferenter sets free the property which has been enjoyed, which is thus held to pass on the death, and this is known as cesser of an interest (see page 116). In general, the death of successive liferenters involves the whole liferented funds in duty on each death (subject to certain exemptions described on page 117) but, on the death of an annuitant, only the part of the property formerly required for payment of the annuity is liable to duty.

Domicile of Deceased.

Where the deceased died domiciled out of Great Britain, only the property in Great Britain is liable. If he died domiciled in Great Britain the situation of property passing on the death is immaterial, except as regards heritable property which is exempt if abroad (sec. 2 (2)). The ascertainment of domicile presents many difficulties and is beyond the scope of this work. Generally speaking it may be said that a person's domicile is in the country where he has his home. If deceased died domiciled abroad, questions may arise as to where property is situated for duty purposes, and the general principles are as follows :—

(1) Shares in companies pass in the country where the company has its head office or keeps its register. If two registers are kept it depends on the situation of the certificates.

(2) Bearer bonds pass in the country in which they are held at the date of death if they are capable of being sold there.

(3) Shares in partnerships are situated where the business is carried on.

(4) Settled property is situated in Great Britain if (*a*) under the will of a person domiciled in Britain, or (*b*) the settlement was originally British, or (*c*) the settlement has become British before the death of the liferenter on whose death the claim for duty has arisen.

(5) Debts are situated where the debtor resides and where proceedings can be taken to enforce payment.

II. Property Deemed to Pass on Death

Under Finance Act, 1894, sec. 2, property is deemed to pass if it falls under any of the following classes :—

(1) *Property of which Deceased was competent to dispose* at his death, which is defined by sec. 22 (2*a*) as including property in which he had such an estate, or interest, or power of appointment, as would enable him to dispose of the property if he were *sui juris*. Persons are *sui juris* if they are legally entitled to enter into contracts and administer their affairs. Those who are not *sui juris* include children and lunatics.

Property falling under this heading includes, for example, (*a*) an interest in expectancy, *i.e.* property vested in the deceased as fiar but held by trustees for the liferent of another person, or (*b*) property held by trustees but over which deceased had a power of appointment, that is, he could dispose of it.

(2) *Donations Mortis Causa, i.e.* death-bed gifts, made in anticipation of the death of the donor, are liable to estate duty on his death.

(3) *Gifts Inter Vivos.*—Gifts made by the deceased within three years of death are liable to duty except in the following cases (see F.A., 1910, sec. 59) :—

(*a*) Gifts for charitable or public purposes made more than one year before death.

(*b*) Gifts in consideration of marriage.

(*c*) " Reasonable " gifts forming part of deceased's normal expenditure, but not gifts out of capital.

(*d*) Gifts not exceeding £100 to any one person.

(4) *Gifts by Deceased*, of which complete *bona fide* possession was not taken. This covers fictitious gifts where the donor actually retained possession of, or an interest in, the property.

(5) *Property placed in Trust by Deceased* if the trust could have been revoked by him, or if he reserved to himself the income or any part thereof.

(6) *Life Policies.*—Money receivable under life policies is liable ·if these were effected by deceased on his own life and kept up (by payment of premiums) by him for the benefit of another person. If they were kept up by another person for his own benefit the proceeds are not liable to duty on the death of the insured. Fully paid policies given away by the deceased outside the three years' limit are not liable to duty.

(7) *Interests and Annuities* wholly or partly purchased by deceased, for example, (*a*) pensions to which deceased contributed, (*b*) pensions from employers' pension funds, or (*c*) annuities purchased by him for others, of which payment commences at his death. Widows' pensions payable by the State are not chargeable, nor are voluntary gifts of pensions.

(8) *Property formerly liferented by Deceased* if surrendered within three years of death (one year if surrendered in favour of charitable or public trusts). This includes surrender on bankruptcy or re-marriage. (F.A., 1900, sec. 11, and F.A., 1910, sec. 59.) See also F.A., 1930, sec. 39, as to annuities surrendered to the fiar.

(9) *Cesser of Interests.*—If any person had an annuity or liferent interest which ceased on a death, there is liability to duty on the property set free. It is not essential that the person who died should be the same person as he whose interest ceased. Where the interest which ceased is restricted to a share of the income from settled property, only the proportionate part of the property set free is held to pass. This is known as the Slice Theory. If the whole trust income was payable to deceased the total settled property is liable.

As examples of interests ceasing may be taken (*a*) a trust liferented by deceased until death, or (*b*) a trust liferented by a woman during the life of her husband, or (*c*) trust funds set aside to provide an annuity to deceased during his life.

Slice Theory.   The following example shows the operation of the Slice Theory :—

An annuitant received £140 per annum from trust funds valued at £40,000 on which the total income was £1400. The sum liable is therefore $\frac{140}{1400} \times £40,000 = £4000$. For the purposes of the Slice Theory the net income is taken after deducting repairs and burdens on heritable property. (Lord Advocate *v.* Fothringham, 1924, S.C. 52.)

If for any reason there is difficulty in ascertaining the actual trust income, the average ruling yield of trust investments on the Stock Exchange can be applied to capitalise the annuity. For example, if the yield on government securities is 4% the amount liable in respect of an annuity of £40 is £1000.

Trusts where the income is only payable to the beneficiaries at the *Discretionary Trusts.* discretion of the trustees are known as " Discretionary Trusts " ; for example, trusts where the income is directed to be applied in payment of the cost of maintenance or education of any persons. On the death of one out of several joint recipients of such income, no property passes for duty purposes ; but on the death of the last survivor, when the discretionary trust terminates, the whole fund is held to pass. The reason is that the fund is then completely set free, for the first time.

III. EXEMPTIONS FROM DUTY

Property is not chargeable with duty if it is in any of the following categories :—

(1) Property in which deceased was only interested as holder of an office (such as a treasurer of a society) or recipient of the benefits of a charity (sec. 2 (1b)).

(2) Heritable property situated out of Great Britain (sec. 2 (2)).

(3) Property held by deceased as a trustee (sec. 2 (3)).

(4) On the death of a surviving spouse, settled property which has already borne estate duty, on the death of the other spouse since the date of settlement, is exempt, provided deceased was not competent to dispose of it. (F.A., 1894, sec. 5 (2), and F.A., 1914, sec. 14.) For example, if a husband has died leaving his property in trust for liferent by his wife and then absolutely to his children, no duty is payable on her death if duty has already been charged on his death. But if he leaves his property to his wife absolutely, or settled in such a way that she has a power of appointment over it, duty is again chargeable on the property on her death.

(5) Estates of less than £100 are exempt unless aggregation with other property makes the total over £100 (sec. 8 (1)).

(6) Annuities provided by deceased—a single annuity if less than £25 or the first of such annuities if there are more than one (sec. 15 (1)). This refers to annuities falling under (7) of property deemed to pass (above).

(7) British Government Securities held in beneficial ownership by persons who are not resident in Great Britain, if of the following issues (F.A., 1915 (No. 2), sec. 47) :—

> $3\frac{1}{2}$% War Loan.
> 4% Funding Loan.
> 4% Victory Bonds.
> National Savings Certificates issued before 1/9/22.

This exemption includes stocks liferented by deceased, as liferent is a beneficial ownership for this purpose.

(8) Miscellaneous exemptions are also conferred by F.A., 1894, secs. 3, 5 (3), 8 (1), 15 ; F.A., 1896, secs. 14, 15 ; F.A., 1900, sec. 14 ; F.A., 1910, sec. 61 (5) ; F.A., 1912, sec. 9 ; F.A., 1928, sec. 30 ; F.A., 1930, sec. 40 ; and F.A., 1931, sec. 40.

IV. Valuation of Property

The value at which property is liable is the price which could be obtained in open market at the date of death, except shares in certain private companies which, as explained below, are to be valued according to the value of the total assets of the company (F.A., 1894, sec. 7 (5) ; F.A., 1910, sec. 60 ; F.A., 1930, secs. 37, 38). Joint property is liable on the part provided by deceased. The following notes give details of the basis to be adopted for various types of property.

(1) *Heritable Properties.*—A valuation may conveniently be made by a qualified valuer, although this is not legally necessary and is not binding even if made. It is usual in the first place to estimate the value, keeping in view the value of adjoining property and any other relevant circumstances, leaving the final figure for subsequent negotiation with the Valuation Department of the Inland Revenue. If the property is sold soon after the death, the sale price will generally be adopted as the value.

Special provisions as to agricultural property (including mansion-house and cottages) are given by F.A., 1894, sec. 7 (5) ; F.A., 1910, sec. 61 (1) ; F.A., 1911, sec. 18 ; and F.A., 1925, sec. 23.

(2) *Furniture and Personal Effects.*—It is usual to obtain a detailed valuation by a qualified valuer except in cases where the total value is negligible, when an estimate may be made by the executors.

(3) *Goodwill of Businesses* carried on by deceased, either with or without partners, must be estimated on the basis of the probable sum receivable on a sale allowing for changes following on the death of deceased. Goodwill may be valued in terms of the partnership agreement (see next paragraph).

(4) *Shares in Partnerships* owned by deceased are valued according to the circumstances of each case. There are usually provisions in the agreement for the deceased's share being bought by the surviving partners, and if a fair price can be calculated on this basis that is the value for duty purposes. Alternatively, the capital and accrued profits as shown in the last balance sheet will form the basis subject to adjustment for goodwill if necessary.

(5) *Life Policies.*—Bonuses are included—the value for duty being the total sum receivable under the policies.

(6) *Debts due to Deceased.*—Bad debts are not liable to duty and doubtful debts are liable only on the sums estimated to be recoverable.

(7) *Gifts.*—If *inter vivos* gifts are liable to duty they are chargeable on the value of the property as at the date of death. (See Strathcona *v.* Inland Revenue, 1929, S.C. 800.)

(8) *Investments*—

(a) *Quoted Investments.*—If stocks or shares are quoted on a Stock Exchange, the official list of prices forms the basis of valuation. The list for the date of death is adopted unless that day was a Sunday or Stock Exchange holiday, when the price for the day either before or after is taken. By concession the Estate Duty Office has adopted the quarter difference basis under which a price of 99-100 is taken as $99\frac{1}{4}$, being the lower of the two prices plus one quarter of the difference. The London list should be used whenever there is a quotation there, unless it can be shown that the list of a provincial exchange gives a fairer price owing to more frequent dealings.

In the London Official and Supplementary lists the closing prices are always given, but in provincial lists there are columns also for last price (*i.e.* previous price) and business done, and there may not be entries in all columns. The price for duty purposes in provincial lists is taken primarily from " closing prices " on the quarter difference basis, or, if no closing price, from " business done "—taking the mean (or average) of the quoted dealings. If there is neither closing price nor business done the " last price " should be taken. " Odd lot " prices may be ignored.

If prices are quoted " ex div." the dividend must also be included as an item of estate unless it had been collected by deceased, when it is presumed to be included in the bank balance.

The following notes apply to stocks and shares in which there is not a free market. Where the price quoted is nominal —that is, no actual buyers or sellers, an adjustment to a fair price should be made. If there are actual dealings soon after the death, at a price widely different from the quoted price at the date of death, the Inland Revenue may endeavour to claim the more recent price if it is higher, but conversely the executors should claim it if it is lower.

Advice as to these points should be obtained from a stockbroker.

(b) *Heritable Bonds, Terminable Debentures or Deposits.*—If deceased had lent money on bond or debenture, or had made deposits repayable at a fixed date, it is usual to include these at par plus interest accrued since the last date of payment (less tax). This basis is subject to negotiation with the Inland Revenue, and if there is any question as to the insufficiency of funds to meet capital or interest a deduction should be claimed. If the rate of interest on loans, which are not yet due for repayment, is less than the current rate, an allowance may be granted depending on the unexpired period. Heritable bonds subject to the Rent etc. Restriction Acts may be subject to an allowance accordingly.

(c) *Unquoted Shares in Public Companies.*—The secretary should be asked to state the last price at which a transfer was made and the date of the transaction, and this price will generally be accepted. If no transfers have occurred recently it is necessary to negotiate the value of the shares with the Inland Revenue Authorities, keeping in view the assets and earning power shown in recent years, as for private companies (see below).

If sold soon after death the sale price may be accepted as the basis of valuation.

(d) *Unquoted Shares in Private Companies.*—Owing to the fact that each case must be judged on its own merits it is difficult to give definite guidance as to such shares. There are two methods of approach—the first method being based on capital and the second on income—and a combination of the results of these usually gives a fair value.

In calculating the capital value the question of rights to share in any surplus assets on liquidation must be considered. If there are such rights these must be valued, including goodwill at the sum which might be received on a sale of the business, allowing for changes in profits owing to new fashions, local conditions, and competition in the trade, etc.

As to income, the earnings and dividends for recent years should be noted. If the trend of earnings is moving up or down this affects goodwill (see above). It is important to observe whether dividends have been fully covered by earnings and if an apparently conservative financial basis is maintained. Where the shares in question bear a fixed rate of dividend, the value of the shares depends on the rate earned on trustee securities at the date of valuation, adjusted to allow for the additional risk. Thus when $3\frac{1}{2}\%$ War Loan is at par, an industrial £1 6% preference share of good status should be worth about 24s., thus yielding 5%. If not of fully satisfactory status a deduction may be made. In valuing participating preference or ordinary shares the probable earnings for the next few years must be estimated. These are then capitalised on the basis of say 2% over trustee rate, *i.e.* $5\frac{1}{2}\%$ when $3\frac{1}{2}\%$ War Loan is at par. A £1 share estimated to receive 11% is thus worth £2.

In combining the results an average may generally be taken; thus assuming an ordinary share of £1 to be worth 23s. 6d. on assets basis, and 37s. 6d. on earnings basis, the value may be estimated at 30s. 6d. subject to any special factors.

Leading cases on this subject are Salvesen's Trustees *v.* Commissioners of Inland Revenue (9 A.T.C. 43), Attorney-General *v.* Jameson (1905, 2, Irish Reports 218), and *Re* Paulin (1935, 1 K.B. 26).

(e) *Shares in Companies controlled by Deceased.*—Special rules are provided by F.A., 1930, secs. 37 and 38, for application when the company was controlled by deceased (which for this purpose includes cases where the deceased had the right to more than half of the income of the company) if in addition either (*a*) the company was so constituted as not to be controlled by the shareholders or any class thereof, or (*b*) the company has not issued to the public more than half of the shares controlling it. In such cases the shares are to be valued according to the value of the total assets of the company including goodwill.

This section also applies when the deceased has been in

receipt of " benefits," such as a salary or annuity, from a
company to which he had transferred property in a manner
involving liability under F.A., 1930, sec. 34, but in this case
the sum liable under that section is deducted from the
assets.

This section does not apply to preference shares, or shares
which have been officially quoted in a United Kingdom stock
exchange, or which have been the subject of dealings there.

(f) *Foreign Assets.*—In converting the value of shares quoted
abroad, by concession the quarter difference basis may be
adopted : thus rupees quoted at date of death at 1s. 6d. to
1s. 6½d. are taken at 1s. 6½d. Conversely, it must be noted
that currencies such as dollars and francs which are quoted
at a number of units per £1 are taken at one quarter less than
the higher number : thus $4·86 to $4·87 = $4·86¾, because
a rate of $4·86 gives a higher value to the dollar than $4·87.

Property abroad which is liable to duty may be subject
to an allowance not exceeding 5% for expenses incurred, owing
to its situation, for purposes of administration and realisation
(sec. 7 (3)).

Foreign property which is subject to death duties abroad
is only chargeable to British estate duty on the balance after
deduction of the foreign death duties (sec. 7 (4)).   A different
basis is applicable to property in certain British dominions
and possessions which grant reciprocal relief, as in this case
the duty payable in the dominions, etc., is deducted from the
duty payable here on that property—the limit of relief being
the latter figure (sec. 20 (1)).   If the dominions do not
reciprocate, the property is treated as foreign property as
described above.

Example.—Assuming balances were held in banks in New
York and Montreal amounting to the equivalent of £300 in
each case, if the death duties abroad in both cases are 2% and
the British estate duty is 5%, the duty is calculated thus :—

Estate Duty on New York balance £300
   less duty £6 = £294 at 5% .   .   £14 14 0

Estate Duty on Montreal balance £300
   at 5% £15 0 0
   Less Canadian death duty £300 at 2%   6 0 0

   £9 0 0

V. Aggregation

In ascertaining the rate of duty, the whole estate passing on the
death is aggregated unless falling under exemptions described below
(F.A., 1894, sec. 4, and F.A., 1900, sec. 12).   If there are large trust
funds passing on the death this has the unfortunate effect of involving
small personal estates in high rates of duty, as the scale of duty is steeply
graduated.   In general, each property passing on the death bears its
own duty.

Exemptions
from
Aggregation.

Exemptions from aggregation are as follows :—

(1) Any property passing on the death in which deceased never had an interest. Such property is an estate by itself for duty purposes.

Examples.—(*a*) Life policies on husband's life but expressed to be for wife's benefit, and which would not have reverted to him if she had died first, or (*b*) widow's pension or annuity liable under heading (7) of " property deemed to pass " (see above).

(2) Property exempted from estate duty.
(3) Property given for national purposes on which duty is remitted.
(4) Property passing under the will of deceased if the total is under £1000. This is treated as an estate by itself, and all the other property passing on the death (of which deceased was not competent to dispose) forms a separate estate (sec. 16 (3)).

In computing the total for this purpose the Inland Revenue treat as passing under deceased's will the following :—

(*a*) Annuities, etc., provided by deceased.
(*b*) Interests in provident funds chargeable with duty although deceased had no personal interest.
(*c*) Property over which deceased had, and exercised, a general power of appointment by his will.
(*d*) Donations *mortis causa*.
(*e*) Gifts *inter vivos* if chargeable to duty.

If advantageous to the executors, a fiar's vested interest in a trust subject to liferent is treated in practice as part of the property settled by the deceased's will, for this purpose, although this is not strictly correct. This basis is advantageous if after including such items the total is still under £1000.

Example—
The property liable to duty is—

Property passing under deceased's will . . .	£600
Vested right of fee liable to duty	350
Settled property over which deceased had no power of disposal	3000
	£3950

If strictly charged, the £600 personal estate would be liable for 2% duty = £12 and all the other property would be aggregated giving £3350 which involves 3% duty = £100, 10s. and making total duty £112, 10s.

Under the concessional treatment the property under the will is taken as £950 which is thus liable at 2% = £19, and the other property of £3000 is liable at 3% = £90 making total liability £109, giving a saving of £3, 10s.

(5) Miscellaneous exemptions from aggregation are given by F.A., 1894, sec. 5 ; F.A., 1900, sec. 12 ; F.A., 1912, sec. 9 ; F.A., 1930, secs. 34, 35, 40 ; and Death Duties (Killed in War) Act, 1914, sec. 2.

VI. RATES OF DUTY

The rates of duty at present in force are as given in F.A., 1930, except as regards agricultural property which is chargeable at lower rates per F.A., 1919, as directed by F.A., 1925, sec. 23. The rates for deaths after 1st August 1930 are as follows :—

Where the Principal Value of the Estate—					Estate Duty shall be payable at the Rate per cent. of
Exceeds	£100	and does not exceed		£500	1
„	500	„	„	1,000	2
„	1,000	„	„	5,000	3
„	5,000	„	„	10,000	4
„	10,000	„	„	12,500	5
„	12,500	„	„	15,000	6
„	15,000	„	„	18,000	7
„	18,000	„	„	21,000	8
„	21,000	„	„	25,000	9
„	25,000	„	„	30,000	10
„	30,000	„	„	35,000	11
„	35,000	„	„	40,000	12
„	40,000	„	„	45,000	13
„	45,000	„	„	50,000	14
„	50,000	„	„	55,000	15
„	55,000	„	„	65,000	16
„	65,000	„	„	75,000	17
„	75,000	„	„	85,000	18
„	85,000	„	„	100,000	19
„	100,000	„	„	120,000	20
„	120,000	„	„	150,000	22
„	150,000	„	„	200,000	24
„	200,000	„	„	250,000	26
„	250,000	„	„	300,000	28
„	300,000	„	„	400,000	30
„	400,000	„	„	500,000	32
„	500,000	„	„	600,000	34
„	600,000	„	„	800,000	36
„	800,000	„	„	1,000,000	38
„	1,000,000	„	„	1,250,000	40
„	1,250,000	„	„	1,500,000	42
„	1,500,000	„	„	2,000,000	45
„	2,000,000			...	50

Small estates are allowed certain privileges by F.A., 1894, sec. 16, and F.A., 1910, sec. 61. Thus if the total gross value of property passing under deceased's will before deducting debts is under £300, a fixed stamp duty of £1, 10s. is payable, and if under £500 the duty is £2, 10s. No interest is chargeable on these sums if paid within one year of death, but otherwise interest runs from date of death. If the deduction of debts would considerably reduce the amount of the estate, it may be preferable to pay 1% on the net value.

Example—

Assume the gross estate amounted to £150 and there are debts of £40. It is preferable to pay 1% on £110 = £1, 2s. rather than to pay £1, 10s. fixed duty.

In ascertaining the gross estate for purpose of claiming fixed duty, there are included the same classes of property as in claiming exemption from aggregation No. 4 (above).

Marginal Relief.

Where the amount of the estate liable to duty is relatively little in excess of one of the limits on the scale of duties, thus involving a higher rate of duty over the whole property, the executors have the option to pay the duty on that limit figure, plus the amount of the estate in excess of the limit. This is an advantage and should be claimed if this is less than the duty calculated in the ordinary way. (F.A., 1914, sec. 13 (1)).

Example—

Estates not exceeding £30,000 pay 10% and between £30,000 and £35,000 pay 11%.

An estate of £30,200 at 11% would be liable for £3322, but on taking advantage of marginal relief the duty would be 10% on £30,000 = £3000 plus £200 = £3200.

The relief is apportionable rateably over the whole aggregable property so that each part receives a share of it.

The marginal limits with 1930 rates of duty are as follows :—

Where the Principal Value of the Estate—				Maximum Amount of Estate to which Sec. 13 (1) of Finance Act, 1914, applies.		
				£	s.	d.
Exceeds	£100	and does not exceed	£500	101	0	3
,,	500	,, ,,	1,000	505	2	0
,,	1,000	,, ,,	5,000	1,010	6	2
,,	5,000	,, ,,	10,000	5,052	1	8
,,	10,000	,, ,,	12,500	10,105	5	3
,,	12,500	,, ,,	15,000	12,632	19	7
,,	15,000	,, ,,	18,000	15,161	5	10
,,	18,000	,, ,,	21,000	18,195	13	1
,,	21,000	,, ,,	25,000	21,230	15	5
,,	25,000	,, ,,	30,000	25,277	15	7
,,	30,000	,, ,,	35,000	30,337	1	7
,,	35,000	,, ,,	40,000	35,397	14	7
,,	40,000	,, ,,	45,000	40,459	15	5
,,	45,000	,, ,,	50,000	45,523	5	1
,,	50,000	,, ,,	55,000	50,588	4	9
,,	55,000	,, ,,	65,000	55,654	15	3
,,	65,000	,, ,,	75,000	65,783	2	8
,,	75,000	,, ,,	85,000	75,914	12	8
,,	85,000	,, ,,	100,000	86,049	7	8
,,	100,000	,, ,,	120,000	101,250	0	0
,,	120,000	,, ,,	150,000	123,076	18	6
,,	150,000	,, ,,	200,000	153,947	7	4
,,	200,000	,, ,,	250,000	205,405	8	1
,,	250,000	,, ,,	300,000	256,944	8	11
,,	300,000	,, ,,	400,000	308,571	8	7
,,	400,000	,, ,,	500,000	411,764	14	1
,,	500,000	,, ,,	600,000	515,151	10	4
,,	600,000	,, ,,	800,000	618,750	0	0
,,	800,000	,, ,,	1,000,000	825,806	9	0
,,	1,000,000	,, ,,	1,250,000	1,033,333	6	8
,,	1,250,000	,, ,,	1,500,000	1,293,103	9	0
,,	1,500,000	,, ,,	2,000,000	1,581,818	3	8
,,	2,000,000		...	2,200,000	0	0

In cases of quick succession to land or businesses carried on otherwise than by a company (*i.e.* by partnerships or individuals) relief from duty is given on a subsequent death involving liability on the same property, if deceased took possession on the previous death, as follows :— Relief on Quick Succession.

Where the second death occurs within one year the relief is 50% of the duty, 2 years 40%, 3 years 30%, 4 years 20%, and 5 years 10% (F.A., 1914, sec. 15). If the value for duty purposes has increased at the second death the relief is calculated only on the lower value. No relief is given where the property passing consists of shares in limited companies, but the relief is applicable where deceased was a liferenter and the testator died within 5 years (Warren's Trustees *v.* Lord Advocate, 1928, S.C. 806).

VII. ESTATE DUTY INVENTORIES

Within six months of the date of death the executors must lodge an inventory of the whole property passing on the death, and if additional estate is subsequently discovered an additional inventory must be lodged within two months of the discovery. It is necessary to include all property passing or deemed to pass on the death, less debts due by deceased and funeral expenses.

The capital and accrued profits of each partnership business may be shown in one sum, but all other items of estate must be fully detailed.

Examples of items of estate are houses, furniture, debts due to deceased, uncashed cheques and dividend warrants, pensions, salaries and fees receivable, accrued income on funds liferented, rents accrued to date of death, income tax recoverable, and cash in house. Values are placed on each on the basis explained above.

Deductions are allowed for debts due by deceased, and reasonable funeral expenses. Debts include income tax and sur-tax, rent, rates, feuduty, etc. (see Chapter "Liferent and Fee," page 23). Secured debts are deducted from the property over which they are secured (sec. 7). No allowance is given for debts incurred without full consideration, *e.g.* contributions promised to charities. The cost of a tombstone is also not allowed. If there are partly paid shares which are of no value, calls due on these may be treated as debts.

The following is an example of particulars required for the estate duty inventory for insertion on the official forms A1 and A2 :—

Estate of the late Thomas Jones who died at Edinburgh
on 10th October 1933.

I. MOVEABLE ESTATE—SCOTLAND

Stocks of the U.K.—

1. £400 3½% War Loan at 101½ £406 0 0

Stocks of Companies, etc.—

2. Edinburgh Corporation £100 4½%
   Mortgage at par £100 0 0
   Add accrued int. from 15th May
   1933 (148 days) £1, 16s. 6d.
   less tax 9s. 1d. . . . 1 7 5
                                                       101 7 5

                                              Forward £507 7 5

Forward	£507	7	5
3. Cash at house	5	0	0
4. *Cash at Bankers—*			
Sum at credit of current account with Bank of Scotland, Meadows, Edinburgh	188	9	7
5. *Personal Effects* as per Inventory dated 31st October 1933 by John Smith & Sons, licensed valuers .	22	10	0
Income due—			
6. Income Tax recoverable to date of death . .	17	15	0

7. Accrued income on £4000 3½% War Loan liferented by deceased under Will of late James Jones per account No. 4 annexed. Interest from 1st June 1933 (131 days) £50, 4s. 11d. less tax £12, 11s. 3d.   37   13   8

Total Moveable Estate in Scotland.   .   .   .   £778   15   8

II. MOVEABLE ESTATE—ENGLAND

8. Imperial Chemical Industries Ltd., 200 7% pref. shares at 28s. 6d.   285   0   0

Total Moveable Estate in Great Britain .   .   .   £1063   15   8

SUMMARY OF ACCOUNTS

Inventory Account or Schedule.	Gross Value of Property.	Amount of Debts and Incumbrances.	Net Value of Property.
Moveables—Account No. 1	£1063 15 8	£28 4 2	£1035 11 6
do. 2	...	...	...
do. 3	...	...	...
do. 4	4022 6 4	...	4022 6 4
do. 7	...	...	...
Heritage—Account No. 5	200 0 0	100 0 0	100 0 0

Total Aggregate for determining rate of Estate Duty   .   £5157   17   10

The rate of estate duty is therefore 4%.

    Deduct Any parts of total aggregate in respect of which duty is not *now* paid—

        (*a*) Value of interests in expectancy   .   .   .   Nil

        (*b*) Value of property in A/c No. 4 (assessed on trustees of that property)   .   .   £4022   6   4

        (*c*) Value of property in A/c No. 5 (payable later)   .   100   0   0

                                         4122   6   4

Amount whereon Estate Duty is *now* to be paid   .   .   £1035   11   6

Author's Note.—For simplicity, the calculation of total duty and interest is omitted.

Account No. 1—Amount of moveable estate in Great
Britain per Inventory £1063 15 8

Schedule No. 1—*part* 1—*Funeral Expenses*—
John Wilson & Sons, undertakers £18 10 0
The Scotsman—intimation of death 0 10 0

£19 0 0

Schedule No. 1—*part* 2—*Debts due by deceased*—
Dr Wilson, Edinburgh, professional attendance . . £3 3 0
John Murray, 42 Middle Street, Leith, chemist's
account 1 11 2
Mrs Macnaughton, 10 Meadow Walk, Edinburgh, board
and lodging 4 10 0

£9 4 2
Add amount of part 1 . . . . . 19 0 0

£28 4 2

Account No. 2—Amount of moveable estate outside Great
Britain . . . . Nil
Schedule No. 2—Debts due by deceased outside Great
Britain (to be deducted from estate p. A/c No. 2) . Nil
Account No. 3—Moveable property of which deceased at
the time of his death was competent to dispose but
did not dispose of . . . . . . Nil
Account No. 4—*Moveable property chargeable with Estate
Duty on deceased's death* (other than in Inventory
or Accounts 3 and 6)—
Property liferented by deceased under will of the late
James Jones who died on 10th March 1923—
Trustees William Macdonald and Charles Maxwell—
£4000 3½% War Loan at 101½ £4060 0 0
Less income accrued due to deceased already included
in inventory and not again liable here . . 37 13 8

£4022 6 4
Account No. 5—*Heritable Property*—
House, 1428 High Street, Edinburgh, passing under
deceased's will, estimated at £200 0 0

Note.—Details of rental and burdens to be supplied on Form 16.
Schedule No. 5—*Incumbrances upon Heritable Property in Account No.* 5—
Bond and Disposition in Security dated 10th March 1896
in favour of John Jackson over 1428 High Street,
Edinburgh £100 0 0

Account No. 6—Property chargeable as an estate by itself. Nil
Note.—This applies where aggregation is not required.
Account No. 7—(This is printed separately as form A7 for
corrections required prior to payment of duty) . Nil

VIII. PAYMENT OF DUTY

The duty on moveable property is due on the date of death, and 3% interest is chargeable on unpaid duty from that date. The duty on heritable property is payable in eight yearly instalments or sixteen half-yearly instalments, commencing twelve months after date of death, with 3% interest on the balance due as from the date the first instalment is due. All instalments fall due on the sale of the property if it occurs before the whole duty has been paid (sec. 6).

If there is liability on a vested interest in expectancy in settled property, the executors have the option to postpone payment until it falls into possession (sec. 7 (6)). Estate duty on timber is payable only when sales are effected (F.A., 1912, sec. 9). The duty on annuities may be paid in four annual instalments—the first being due one year after date of death, with 3% interest from the date the first instalment is due (F.A., 1896, sec. 16).

3% discount is allowed on prepayment of any estate duty.

Government securities which have been held by deceased for at least six months prior to his death may be surrendered for duty as follows :—

4% Funding Loan at 80% plus accrued interest since last payment of interest.

4% Victory Bonds at par plus accrued interest since last payment of interest.

If such securities have been held by a partnership shared by deceased they may be surrendered for duty to the extent of the proportion belonging to deceased. When these prices are less than market prices it is, of course, not advisable to surrender securities in this way.

An executor is only liable for duty on funds over which he has control to the extent of assets received by him (sec. 8 (3)). Settled property passing on the death is chargeable with the duty thereon and as a general rule each property bears its own duty. Duty on gifts *inter vivos* (if liable) is chargeable on the recipient (*re* Foster, 1897, 1 Ch. 484), and estate duty on annuities provided by the deceased is payable by the annuitant, unless the contrary is expressed in the will. The estate duty on legacies is usually payable out of the residue of the trust. It is so payable if (1) the legacies are declared to be free of duty, or (2) the legacies are pecuniary legacies payable out of the free moveable estate in Great Britain and the residue is not exhausted (*re* Morrison, 1910, 102, L.T. 530). In other circumstances, which in practice are exceptional, the duty is payable by the legatee. Estate duty is a charge on capital and the interest thereon is payable out of income (*re* Parker-Jervis, 1898, 2 Ch. 643).

Example—

A died leaving property (after deduction of debts) with a net value of £7500. Within three years of death he had given his son investments which at date of his death were valued at £1500. He received income from funds of £1500 in trust under the will of his wife (who had predeceased him). These funds were previously charged with duty on her death and accordingly no further duty is payable thereon on his death.

He also received an annuity of £100 from another trust where the funds were valued at £20,000 and the total income was £800. Duty is payable as follows :—

(1) Aggregation of property passing :

Personal estate	£7,500
Gift to son	1,500
Trust funds applicable to annuity $\dfrac{100}{800} \times £20,000$	2,500
Total estate liable to aggregation . .	£11,500

Note.—Wife's trust is excluded from aggregation as it is not liable.

(2) The rate of duty is 5%—the total being over £10,000 and under £12,500.

(3) Incidence of duty :

Payable by executors—on personal estate £7500 at 5%	£375
Payable by son on gift £1500 at 5% . .	75
Payable by trustees from trust funds £2500 at 5%	125
	£575

CHAPTER XIII

LEGACY DUTY

I. INTRODUCTION

THIS duty is charged in terms of the Legacy Duty Act, 1796 (to which Act the references apply unless otherwise stated). The rates have since been increased, and some exemptions have been withdrawn by subsequent legislation. Legacy duty is payable on death-bed gifts, and legacies of fixed capital sums, or shares of residue, or annuities directed in wills, etc. Sums falling due under an intestacy or by operation of legal rights are liable for duty in the same way as legacies instructed in a will.

Domicile.

Legacy duty is due on legacies from moveable property where the testator was domiciled in Great Britain. Legacies payable out of heritable property are not liable to legacy duty, but instead are liable to Succession Duty (see page 136). Heritable bonds are moveable property for duty purposes. The situation of the funds bequeathed does not affect the liability and thus moveable property in Great Britain is not liable when it is bequeathed by a person domiciled abroad, while conversely moveable property abroad is liable if bequeathed by a person domiciled in Great Britain. (See Thomson v. Advocate General, 13 Sim. 153.)

Legacies Chargeable.

For duty purposes, legacies include (1) a direction to pay the debts of another person, (2) a gift to an executor for his trouble, (3) the forgiveness of a debt due to the testator, (4) the succession duty on a legacy of heritable property left free of duty, (5) donations *mortis causa*, (6) options given by the will to any person to purchase a part of testator's property at less than market value—the " legacy " being the difference in values. As to what legacies are chargeable, see Revenue Act, 1845, sec. 4 ; Foster v. Ley, 1835, 2 Bing. N.C. 269 ; Attorney General v. Holbrook, 1823, 3 Y. and J. 114.

Where powers of appointment are given under wills there may be liability to duty, but many complications arise as to the basis which accordingly is beyond the scope of this chapter.

II. EXEMPTIONS

(1) *Specific Legacies*—

Legacies of specific articles under £20 in value are exempt unless pecuniary legacies to the same legatee bring the total over £20 (44 Vic. C. 12, sec. 42).

(2) *Duty on Free of Duty Legacies*—

Money left to pay duty on a legacy out of some other fund is exempt (Legacy Duty Act, sec. 21). Thus the duty on a legacy of " £300 " is the same as the duty on a legacy of " £300 free of duty," although in one case the legatee receives £270 and in the other £300, assuming the rate of duty is 10%.

The residue of a trust cannot be free of duty as there is no other fund which can bear the duty, but a share of residue may be free, in which case the other share bears all the duty.

(3) *Small Estates—*

These are exempt where the value of the whole moveable estate is less than £100 (43 Vic. C. 14, sec. 13). If the net value of property passing under the will (excluding other property passing on the death) is less than £1000 there is no liability to duty, and marginal relief is given if the total is slightly over £1000 (F.A., 1894, sec. 16 (3), and F.A., 1914, sec. 13 (2)). For this purpose, the property passing under the will is computed in the same way as for estate duty aggregation exemption (see above). This marginal relief applies to legacy duty and succession duty taken together so that the total of these duties does not exceed the estate over £1000.

(4) *If the Principal Value of the Property passing on the Death is under* £15,000, excluding (1) property in which deceased never had an interest, and (2) property of which deceased never was competent to dispose, and which on his death passes to persons other than the husband, wife, lineal ancestor or lineal descendant of the deceased. In the above circumstances legacies to husband, wife, lineal ancestors (*e.g.* parents and grandparents) or lineal descendants (*e.g.* children and grandchildren) are exempt, but other legacies are liable at the usual rates (F.A., 1910, sec. 58 (2)).

(5) *Legacies to Wife and Children of Deceased who are under 21—*

Even if the total estate is over £15,000, so that (4) does not apply, if the amount of the legacies and successions falling to any one of the above persons is less than £2000, no legacy duty is payable on these (F.A., 1910, sec. 58 (2)). If one receives over £2000 he is liable, but any others who receive less than £2000 each are exempt.

(6) *Legacies to Husband, Lineal Ancestors or Lineal Descendants—*

Even if the total estate is over £15,000 so that (4) does not apply, if the amount of the legacies and successions falling to any of the above persons is less than £1000, no legacy duty is payable on these (F.A., 1910, sec. 58 (2)). If one receives over £1000 he is liable, but the others who receive less than £1000 are exempt.

(7) Legacies disclaimed by the legatee are exempt.

(8) See also miscellaneous exemptions p. Legacy Duty Act, 1796, sec. 14 ; Stamp Act, 1815, Sch. III. ; F.A., 1910, sec. 96 ; F.A., 1930, sec. 40.

III. Valuation of Legacies for Duty

Legacy duty is payable on the value of the legacy at the date when it is paid, calculated in the same way as for estate duty purposes. (See Attorney General *v.* Cavendish (Wight, 82).) Sec. 23 deals with legacies compounded for less than full value. If a legacy is payable with interest, the interest is an additional legacy for duty purposes. For example, if payment of a legacy of £100 is delayed for two years and bears interest at 5%, the beneficiary is *prima facie* entitled to £110, and duty is charged on £110, not £100.

Annuities.

Annuities are valued as shown by tables appended to the Succession Duty Act, 1853, which give present capitalised values on an actuarial basis. If the annuities are free of tax, the tax is treated as an additional annuity calculated on the estimated liability (sec. 11). If the will directs that a specified sum be invested in an annuity, that sum is chargeable and the Succession Duty Act tables are not used. Liferent interests are treated as annuities of the amount of the estimated income (sec. 12). In estimating the income where the funds have not been re-invested following realisation by the executors, the current rate obtainable on trustee securities may be adopted. In other cases the income on the specific investments can generally be estimated.

Liferent
Interests.

If the legacy consists of income under a discretionary trust, the amount payable to the beneficiary cannot be stated in advance, and it is necessary to lodge annual statements of actual payments to the beneficiary, on which sums duty is then payable (sec. 11). Voluntary allowances are chargeable in this way (re Northcliffe, 1929, 1 Ch. 327).

As an example of valuation of an annuity, assume that on the death of A an annuity of £3000 is payable to his sister B, aged 52. As shown in Succession Duty Act tables an annuity to a person of that age is valued at £1185, 14s.% = £35,571. 5% duty is payable = £1778, 11s.

IV. LEGACIES OF LIFERENTS

The assessment of a legacy of a liferent is made in one of the following ways :—

(A) If there is only one rate of legacy duty applicable to (1) the first liferenter, (2) any succeeding liferenters, and (3) the residuary legatees, i.e. if all are of the same degree of relationship to the testator, duty is payable on the whole fund as soon after the testator's death as the total can be ascertained. In this case no further liability to legacy duty arises on the deaths of liferenters. (See V. below as to estate liable.)

(B) On the other hand if different rates of duty are applicable to the successive beneficiaries, duty is payable on the value of the first liferent calculated on the annuity basis, per Succession Duty Act tables, and further duty is payable on his death (see below).

(C) If the whole fund passes to the residuary legatee on the death of the first liferenter, duty is then payable on the whole fund, subject to deduction of (1) estate duty payable on the death, (2) accrued income due to the executors of the deceased liferenter, and (3) expenses of division of the residue. If the residue is divisible among various beneficiaries, each pays at the appropriate rate on his own share of the residue.

(D) If there are successive liferents, duty is charged on the death of the first liferenter either (1) on the whole fund—computed under method (C), or (2) on the value of the next liferent—computed under method (B). The first method is used if the same rate of duty is applicable to all succeeding liferenters and the residuary legatees, and no further duty is then payable on deaths of subsequent liferenters. If various rates of duty apply to these persons the annuity method must be used. In the latter case further duty is payable on the death of the second liferenter in the same way, and so on until method (C) is applicable.

Example

A trust fund producing £200 p.a. income is left by R to a charity in fee, subject to liferent first by his sister S, and on her death by his brother T. The liferents are stated to be free of duty.

On R's death his sister S is aged 60, and an annuity of £200 to a person of that age is valued at £972, 1s.% = £1944, 2s. on which duty is payable at 5% = £97, 4s. 1d. This is chargeable against capital, as the liferent is free of duty. On the death of S, T is aged 72, and assuming the income remains at £200 p.a. the value at £623, 19s. 6d.% = £1247, 19s. on which 5% duty = £62, 7s. 11d., payable out of capital as before.

On the death of each liferenter there is also liability for estate duty, but for simplicity it is not shown in this example.

On death of T, 10% duty is payable on the residue, calculated as shown in paragraph (C).

V. LEGACIES OF RESIDUE

Various difficulties arise in calculating the value for duty purposes of legacies of the residue of executry estates. In general terms the gross residue consists of the following :—

(1) Estate retained unchanged—*i.e.* not realised since date of death of deceased—is included at the value at the date when the residuary account is prepared.

(2) Estate which was held at date of death, but since realised, is taken at the realised value. Government securities surrendered for duty are liable at the value at which they were taken over.

(3) Investments made since date of death are included in the residue at the value when the residue is ascertained, but a deduction is allowed of the actual cost of these investments. In effect, increases in value are included but decreases are allowable as deductions.

(4) Income received between date of death and date of residuary account.

Deductions from Residue are as follows :—

(1) Estate duty.

(2) Dues of confirmation.

(3) Funeral expenses.

(4) Debts due by deceased. In addition to debts allowable for estate duty it is permissible to deduct the so-called " voluntary debts," such as annuities payable under bonds granted by deceased without money consideration, if these are binding on the executors.

(5) Expenses of administration.

(6) Legacies, and legacy duty thereon if payable free of duty. This includes annuities separately assessed to legacy duty.

I 2

    (7) Cost of tombstone if directed in will.

    (8) Payments out of income, such as annuities, or interest on loans, debts, duties or legacies.

VI. Rates of Duty

The rate of duty depends on the relationship between the deceased and the legatee. The adoption of children under statutory powers creates a legal relationship, but illegitimate children are liable at 10%—the maximum rate—unless subsequently legitimated by marriage of the parents. A divorced spouse is also liable at 10%. Where the legatee was married to a person who is of nearer relationship to the testator, the lower rate of duty which would apply to the spouse is chargeable, and this is not affected by the death or divorce of that spouse (Bullmore *v.* Wynter, 1883, 22 Ch. D. 619). The relatives of the husband or wife of the deceased are " strangers in blood " and pay the maximum rate.

The present rates of duty are as follows :—

    (1) Where the legatee is the husband, wife, lineal ancestor, or lineal descendant of the deceased—1%.

    (2) Where the legatee is a brother or sister of the deceased or a descendant of these—5%.

    (3) All others—10%.

VII. Date of Payment of Duty

Legacy duty on liferents or annuities, except on sums set aside for purchase of annuities, is payable in four equal annual instalments, the first due twelve months after the annuity begins. If the annuitant dies, or the annuity ceases for other reasons before all the instalments fall due, no further instalments are chargeable (sec. 8). Thus if legacy duty totalling £100 was due in four instalments of £25 each and the annuitant died before the third instalment became payable, only £50 is paid in all.

All other legacy duties are payable when the legacy is set aside or paid. (As to this see Lord Advocate *v.* Wotherspoon's Trustees, 1930, S.L.T. 82.) Advances to residuary legatees are chargeable when paid.

Duty on a legacy of an annuity directed to be purchased is due in one sum. Unless such an annuity is left free of duty, the legacy duty is recovered from the annuitant by purchasing an annuity reduced in proportion to the duty. For example, an annuity of £50 payable to a nephew is taken as actually £47, 10s. as 5% duty is payable.

If legacy duties are chargeable on cessation of a liferent, the duty becomes due on the date of death of the liferenter.

Interest on duty in arrear is payable at 3% and similar discount is allowed on prepayments. If legacy duty due in instalments on an annuity had been prepaid, and the annuitant died before all instalments fell due, the duty overpaid is recoverable (sec. 8).

Government securities may be surrendered for legacy duty as for estate duty.

VIII. Incidence of Duty

While the executor is primarily liable for duty he may recover it from the legatees, unless the legacies are specifically free of duty. The duty on liferents or annuities assessed on the annuity basis is payable by the liferenters or annuitants unless the contrary is stated in the will. Where trust funds are liferented and assessable under method IV (A) above, the duty is chargeable to capital. The residue of a trust cannot be free of duty but a share of residue may be free.

If legacies are bequeathed free of duty, but the estate is insufficient to pay the legacies in full, they are abated and the duty is payable out of the legacies (*re* Turnbull, 1905, 1 Ch. 726).

CHAPTER XIV

SUCCESSION DUTY

I. Introduction

SUCCESSION duty is charged in terms of the Succession Duty Act, 1853, as amended by subsequent Finance Acts. This duty may be considered as a supplementary legacy duty, devised to bring into charge legacies and gifts otherwise exempt. Legacy duty does not charge heritable property, and in general is payable only on legacies under wills or intestacies, but succession duty is payable whenever there is a transfer of property on a death. It therefore operates principally in respect of (1) heritable property passing under a will or on intestacy (such property not being liable for legacy duty), and (2) all settled property passing on a death which is not part of deceased's estate, *e.g.* funds settled by him in a marriage trust. Thus on the death in Scotland of a man owning heritable and moveable estate in Great Britain and who also enjoyed a liferent of settled property, there is liability (1) to estate duty on the *whole* property, (2) to legacy duty on his *moveable* property, (3) to succession duty on his *heritable* property, and (4) to succession duty on the *settled* property.

Successions Chargeable.

Before liability to succession duty can arise there must be a death on which property is transferred, and the transfer must be (*a*) gratuitous —*i.e.* no payment is made by the successor—and (*b*) effected either by disposition—*i.e.* legal deed conveying it to the successor—or by devolution of law, *e.g.* on intestacy.

As regards the situation of property liable to duty, if it is heritable the property must be in Great Britain, and if moveable it must be held under wills or settlements administered in Britain. The domicile of the predecessor and successors does not affect the position.

Owing to the complexity of the duty it is impossible to give here more than an outline of its scope. In the following paragraphs are noted the principal points arising in the assessments.

II. Exemptions

The following property is exempt from succession duty :—

(1) Legacies exempt from legacy duty (sec. 18).
(2) Property already charged to legacy duty on the same death (sec. 18).
(3) Money left to pay succession duty in " free of duty " successions. (See legacy duty exemption No. 2 for explanation.)
(4) Small estates are exempted as for legacy duty (see legacy duty exemption No. 3).
(5) Where the property passing on the death is under £15,000 calculated as for legacy duty exemption No. 4 the same relief

is allowed. Reliefs are also given for legacies under £2000 to wife and children, and £1000 to husband, lineal ancestors or lineal descendants, as for legacy duty exemptions Nos. 5 and 6.

(6) See also miscellaneous exemptions p. Succession Duty Act, sec. 32 ; F.A., 1910, secs. 61 (5), and 96 ; F.A., 1930, sec. 40.

III. Valuation of Successions

The basis of valuation of heritable property depends on whether or not the successor is competent to dispose of the property. (See page 115 for definition of this.) Where the successor is a liferenter who is not competent to dispose of the property, his interest is valued as a life annuity of the amount of the free annual income (sec. 22). Expenses of heritable property are allowed as deductions, including insurance, but excluding income tax and management. Tables are appended to the Succession Duty Act which are applied in valuing annuities, giving the capitalised present values. Heritable property of which the successor is competent to dispose is valued as for estate duty purposes, but deductions are allowed for estate duty payable on the same death and expenses of raising and paying that duty (F.A., 1894, sec. 18). *Heritable Property.*

Moveable property liable to succession duty is charged on the same basis of valuation as for legacy duty purposes (Succession Duty Act, sec. 32). *Moveable Property.*

IV. Rates of Duty

The rates of duty depend on the relationship of the predecessor and successor at the time the succession is conferred, and they are the same rates as are applied in charging legacy duty. It must be noted that a succession is conferred when the relative deed is executed, or on the death of the testator (if under a will), but duty is not necessarily payable at that time. Duty is payable when the succession is held to arise, usually when the successor takes possession. (See F.A., 1925, sec. 24.)

Difficulty may be found in the fact that the predecessor is not necessarily the person on whose death the succession arises. The donor or testator from whom the succession arises is the predecessor for duty purposes, and the person on whom the property is conferred is the successor. Thus if A leaves heritable property to B in liferent and to C in fee, duty is first payable on A's death—A being the predecessor and B the successor. Further duty is payable on B's death—A again being predecessor, but C now being successor. Even if the successor has assigned his rights, duty is usually chargeable as if he had not done so (see sec. 15). *Predecessor and Successor.*

V. Payment of Duty

3% interest is charged on duty unpaid at the due date and 3% discount is allowed on prepayment of duty. Certain Government securities may be surrendered in payment of duty under the same conditions as apply to estate duty.

The due date of payment depends on whether or not the successor is competent to dispose of the property, as follows :—

(1) *Duty on Heritable Property of which the Successor is competent to dispose.*—The duty is payable by eight equal yearly instalments or sixteen half-yearly instalments, the first due twelve months after the successor is entitled to possession (F.A., 1894, sec. 18).

The death of the successor before payment of all the duty does not affect the liability.

(2) *Duty on Heritable Property of which the Successor is* not *competent to dispose.*—The duty is payable either (a) *by eight equal half-yearly instalments*—the first due twelve months after the successor is entitled to possession (sec. 21)—or (b) *at the successor's option* (51 Vic. C. 8, sec. 22).

$\frac{1}{8}$ of duty twelve months after possession.
$\frac{1}{8}$ do.   two years   do.
$\frac{1}{8}$ do.   three years   do.
$\frac{5}{8}$ do.   four years   do.   (or if desired only $\frac{1}{8}$ after four years and then $\frac{1}{8}$ of duty after five years, $\frac{1}{8}$ of duty after six years, $\frac{1}{8}$ of duty after seven years, and $\frac{1}{8}$ of duty after eight years.)

In the event of the successor dying before the due date of the last instalment calculated under method (*a*) no further instalments are chargeable, and, if method (*b*) had been adopted, adjustments to the same effect are made. Under method (*b*) if only $\frac{1}{8}$ duty is paid after four years expire, 3% interest is chargeable from that date on the unpaid balance. If there are successive liferents this method of calculating liability is used in each case, and on the death of the last liferenter paragraph (1) applies.

(3) *Duty on Moveable Property of which the Successor is competent to dispose.*—Duty is payable when the successor is entitled to possession (sec. 32).

(4) *Duty on Moveable Property of which the Successor is* not *competent to dispose.*—Duty is payable in four equal annual instalments —the first due twelve months after the successor is entitled to possession. If the successor dies before all the instalments fall due, the instalments due after date of death are cancelled (sec. 32). In the event of the liferenters and fiars all being chargeable at the same rate of duty, succession duty is charged on the whole property at the beginning of the liferent and no further duty is payable on deaths of liferenters. This basis is similar to that adopted for legacy duty on liferents (see page 132).

(5) *Duty on Timber* is not payable until sale of the timber (F.A., 1910, sec. 61 (5), and F.A., 1912, sec. 9).

VI. Incidence of Duty

The duty is payable by the person who is then entitled to possession of the property charged with duty. Duty on moveable property subject to liferent, where liferenters and fiars are all liable at the same rate, is chargeable to capital. Duty on the succession of a liferenter or annuitant assessed on the annuity basis is usually paid by the trustees who should recover it from the liferenter or annuitant. If, however, in terms of a will a succession is free of duty, the duty may be payable out of the residue of the predecessor's trust funds, or as otherwise directed.

CHAPTER XV

SCHEMES OF DIVISION

When Required.

INTERIM schemes of division may be necessary if part of the residue of a trust is to be handed over to the beneficiaries—the remainder being retained to meet annuities or other sums payable in terms of the will. Another type of interim scheme of division is required where there is a provision in the will for setting aside for liferent some part of the trust funds, so that it is necessary to allocate specific investments for the purpose.

Final schemes of division are required in executry estates where there are several beneficiaries, and where the executors divide the funds after they are satisfied that all debts, duties and legacies have been paid. In trusts the final division is deferred until all the trust purposes are completed, and so the division is made after the death of the last annuitant or liferenter. The balance of income due to the executors of such deceased beneficiary must be paid or reserved before any division is made.

A certificate should be obtained from the Inspector of Taxes that no income tax remains unpaid, before paying over this balance.

Deductions from Estate.

Government duties may be payable on the death of an annuitant or liferenter, and before dividing trust funds a clearance certificate should be obtained from the Estate Duty Office.

An account should be prepared showing the whole cash transactions up to the date of division, and in this account it is convenient to show the expenses of winding up the trust—reserving a sum to cover unpaid items. On each transfer of stock or shares to beneficiaries there is a stamp duty of 10s. (except on transfers of British Government securities which are exempt) and usually also a registration fee of 2s. 6d. Particulars of registration fees charged by companies are given in *The Stock Exchange Official Year Book*. Stamp duties and recording dues are payable in respect of dispositions of heritable property and discharges by beneficiaries. Solicitors and factors are entitled to fees for realisation of the estate, adjustment of government duties, and preparation of account, scheme of division, transfers, dispositions of property, and discharge by beneficiaries. If there is to be an audit, the auditor's fee must be taken into account also.

Division of Investments.

It is frequently more convenient and economical to divide the investments among the beneficiaries instead of realising them on the Stock Exchange and paying out cash. Where a division of investments is made, these must all be revalued as at the date of the division. It is recommended that the expenses of division should all be charged against the trust, instead of allocating them to the beneficiaries individually, although the latter method is sometimes adopted.

Valuation of Funds.

In revaluing the trust funds for division, quoted investments are taken either at middle prices in stock exchange lists, or on the estate duty

140

basis (see page 118), but values of unquoted investments must be estimated. Prices of such shares on recent transfers may sometimes be obtained from the secretary or auditor of the company, but these are not conclusive and the following points must also be taken into account :—

(a) Estate duty office valuation for death duty purposes.

(b) Recent earning capacity, reserves and goodwill, as shown in the accounts.

(c) Restrictions on transfers of shares in terms of articles.

If any shares are quoted x.d., the dividend must also be included in the funds for division, even if it is receivable at a later date.

If each beneficiary receives an equal holding no hardship can arise to anyone, even if the value of the shares is afterwards found to have been wrongly estimated. It is therefore preferable where possible to divide each investment into as many parts as there are beneficiaries, except perhaps for rounding off holdings. For example, 1000 shares divided among three beneficiaries might be taken as 350, 325 and 325. There may be restrictions in the company's articles as to the minimum number of shares or units of stock transferable, and before transfers are prepared enquiry should be made on this point. Where the investments are too small to divide, each beneficiary may be given small lots in different companies. Heritable properties are sometimes taken by individual beneficiaries in order to avoid difficulties through joint ownership. In order to preserve an equitable basis, care must be taken to give each beneficiary investments of approximately equal status— *not* giving one nothing but government stocks and another nothing but ordinary shares. *Basis of Allocation.*

If advances have been made to residuary legatees, interest should be calculated on these sums for the period to the date of division, and the advances and interest together form part of the available residue and are deducted from the respective beneficiaries, thus :— *Advances.*

Previous advances to A (including interest) . .	£300
do. B do. . .	200
Cash available for division	480
	———
Total funds	£980
	═══

A's share ½ = £490

whereof previously advanced . . .	£300
do. cash payable . . .	190
	———
	£490

B's share ½ = £490

whereof previously advanced . . £200	
do. cash payable . . 290	
	—— 490
	———
	£980
	═══

If any beneficiary has already received more than is due to him,

and the excess cannot be recovered from any source, his advances must
be excluded and the remaining estate is then divisible among the others,
thus :—

Funds per accounts—

Advances to A	£400
do. B	90
Cash	750
	£1240

There are four beneficiaries with equal shares.

    A's share ¼ = £310 is less than the sum advanced. If the excess
is not recoverable, the funds are therefore divisible among the
remainder as follows :—

B's share 1/3rd of £840 = ...		£280
whereof advances . . .	£90	
do. cash payable . .	190	
	£280	

C's share 1/3rd of £840 (cash)		280
D's share do. do.		280
		£840

Legal
Questions.
    In dividing the funds of any executry or trust it is necessary to keep
in view the legal rights of the surviving spouse and family of the deceased
unless these have been previously waived or discharged. The executors
or trustees should also be satisfied that every legatee named in the
will or claiming under the law of intestate succession is satisfactorily
identified, and that death has actually occurred of those whose legacies
appear to have lapsed through their predeceasing the testator.

Procedure.
    The proposed division of the estate should first be shown in a draft
scheme of division prepared by the factor, and after approval by the
executors or trustees this may conveniently be submitted to the
beneficiaries for comment. If an audit is required the scheme should
then be submitted to the auditor with the final accounts of the trust
before payments are made to beneficiaries. The auditor may, if desired,
check the transfers of stocks and shares before they are signed. After
the auditor has made his report, further adjustments may be required,
and the final scheme of division is then prepared and submitted to the
trustees and beneficiaries along with transfers and discharge for
signature. The factor then arranges for stamping and registration of
the transfers, and when certificates are received for the sub-divided
investments he must deliver these to the beneficiaries along with any
cash balances.

    Dividends may be received by the factor after the date of division of
the investments before the transfers are lodged, and these sums must be
paid over to the respective beneficiaries.

The following examples show different types of schemes of division :— Examples.

Example I

The annexed scheme of division commences with the funds shown at close of the trust account included in the chapter "Examples of Trust Accounts showing Apportionments " (p. 108).

SCHEME OF DIVISION of the Trust Estate
of the late J. Jones.
As at 31st December 1941.

Estate as revalued per Account Charge and Discharge—

	£	s.	d.
1. £10,000 ord. stock CD Co. Ltd., at 115%	£11,500	0	0
2. £10,000 ord. stock EF Co. Ltd., at 127½%	12,750	0	0
3. £10,000 ord. stock GH Co. Ltd., at 142%	14,200	0	0
4. £20,000 5% deb. stock XX Ltd., at 90%	18,000	0	0
5. £15,000 5% partic. pref. stock YY Ltd., at 101%	15,150	0	0
6. £20,000 5% pref. stock WW Ltd., at 83¾%	16,750	0	0
7. Furniture and personal effects	650	0	0
8. Advances to T. Jones on account of residue	1,000	0	0
9. Advances to J. Wilson on account of residue	500	0	0
	£90,500	0	0
Add Balance at credit with Agents	1,800	7	4
	£92,300	7	4

Note.—Interest has been received on advances to the beneficiaries up to the date of division.

Divisible thus :—

	£	s.	d.
T. Jones—one-third	£30,766	15	10
J. Wilson— „	30,766	15	9
C. Smith— „	30,766	15	9
	£92,300	7	4

	T. Jones.				J. Wilson.				C. Smith.			
	Holding.	Value.			Holding.	Value.			Holding.	Value.		
0,000 ord. stock CD Co. Ltd.	£3,340	£3,841	0	0	£3,330	£3,829	10	0	£3,330	£3,829	10	0
0,000 ord. stock EF Co. Ltd.	3,330	4,245	15	0	3,340	4,258	10	0	3,330	4,245	15	0
0,000 ord. stock GH Co. Ltd.	3,330	4,728	12	0	3,330	4,728	12	0	3,340	4,742	16	0
0,000 5% deb. stock XX Ltd.	6,670	6,003	0	0	6,665	5,998	10	0	6,665	5,998	10	0
5,000 5% partic. pref. stock YY Ltd.	5,000	5,050	0	0	5,000	5,050	0	0	5,000	5,050	0	0
0,000 5% pref. stock WW Ltd.	6,665	5,581	18	9	6,670	5,586	2	6	6,665	5,581	18	9
urniture and personal effects	...	300	0	0	...	200	0	0	...	150	0	0
lvances to T. Jones	...	1,000	0	0	...	......	...	...	...	......	...	...
lvances to J. Wilson	...	......	...	...	...	500	0	0	...	......	...	...
		£30,750	5	9		£30,151	4	6		£29,598	9	9
ish		16	10	1		615	11	3		1,168	6	0
		£30,766	15	10		£30,766	15	9		£30,766	15	9

Example II

In the following example it is assumed that the last trust account was made up to 30th April 1934 and that the liferenter died on 10th September 1934. No further death duties were payable on his death and the estate is to be divided as at 31st December 1934.

The account showed the trust funds as at 30th April 1934 to be as follows :—

£1800 3½% War Loan.
£500 3½% Conversion Loan.
Deposit Receipt with Bank of Scotland dated 15th July 1933 p. £17, 16s. 10d.
Cash balance at credit with factor £12, 16s. 3d., whereof capital 11s. 8d. and income £12, 4s. 7d.

Since the close of that account £15 was paid to the liferenter on 1st July 1934.

STATEMENT OF ACCRUED INCOME due to the deceased JAMES JOHNSTON from Mrs Johnston's Trust as at date of death—10th September 1934.

Balance of income as at 30th April 1934					£12	4	7
Add Interest received—							
½ year's interest on £1800 3½% War Loan to 1st June 1934 .					31	10	0
Note.—Tax reserved below.							
					£43	14	7
Add Interest accrued—							
On £1800 3½% War Loan from 1st June to 10th September 1934 (101 days) £17, 8s. 8d. less tax £3, 18s. 5d.	£13	10	3				
On £500 3½% Conversion Loan from 1st April to 10th September 1934 (162 days) £7, 15s. 4d. less tax £1, 14s. 11d.	6	0	5				
On Deposit Receipt p. £17, 16s. 10d. from 15th July 1933 to 10th September 1934 per Bank certificate 4s. less tax 11d. . . .	0	3	1				
					19	13	9
Note.—Income tax deducted from apportionments (see page 51).					£63	8	4
Less Payment on account on 1st July 1934 . .	£15	0	0				
Sum reserved for income tax at 4s. 6d. per £ on £31, 10s. War Loan interest received 1st June 1934	7	1	9				
Management Expenses—proportion of agent's fees applicable to income	2	2	0				
					24	3	9
Balance of income paid to Executors on 30th October 1934 . .					£39	4	7

STATEMENT OF RECEIPTS AND PAYMENTS by
John Thomson as agent for the Trustees of the late
Mrs Elizabeth Johnston.

From 30th April 1934
To 31st December 1934.
(Close of Trust.)

RECEIPTS

I. Income Received :—
1. *On £1800 3½% War Loan*—
1934.

	£	s.	d.
June 1. ½ yr's int. (no tax deducted)	£31	10	0
Dec. 1. Do. Do.	£31	10	0
	£63	0	0

2. *On £500 3½% Conversion Loan*—
1934.

	£	s.	d.
Oct. 1. ½ yr's int. £8, 15s. less tax £1, 19s. 4d. . .	6	15	8

3. *On Deposit Receipt*—
1934.

	£	s.	d.
Dec. 20. Int. on Deposit Receipt p. £17, 16s. 10d. from 15th July 1933	0	4	8
	£70	0	4

II. Deposit Receipt Uplifted :—
1934.

	£	s.	d.
Dec. 20. Deposit Receipt with Bank of Scotland dated 15th July 1933	17	16	10
Total Receipts	£87	17	2

PAYMENTS

I. Mr James Johnston (deceased)—the liferenter :—
1934.

	£	s.	d.
July 1. Sum paid on account of income	£15	0	0
Oct. 30. Balance of income to 10th September 1934 (date of death) paid to his Executors	39	4	7
	£54	4	7

II. Income Tax :—
1934.

	£	s.	d.
Dec. 31. Sum reserved to meet income tax on £63 War Loan int. and 4s. 8d. Deposit Receipt int. = £63, 4s. 8d. at 4s. 6d.	14	4	7

III. Management and Legal Expenses :—
1934.

	£	s.	d.	£	s.	d.
Dec. 31. John Thomson—fee for preparation of account, scheme of division, transfers, and discharge by beneficiaries, restricted to 25 guineas	£26	5	0			
Do. posts and outlays .	0	10	0			
Reserved to meet stamp on discharge and recording dues thereof . .	2	0	0			
				28	15	0
Total Payments				£97	4	2

K

SUMMARY

	£	s	d
Balance at credit with agent as at 30th April 1934	£12	16	3
Add Receipts	87	17	2
	£100	13	5
Less Payments	97	4	2
Balance at credit with agent as at 31st December 1934 . . .	£3	9	3

SCHEME OF DIVISION of the Estate of the late Mrs ELIZABETH JOHNSTON as at 31st December 1934.

	£	s	d
Estate as revalued at this date :—			
£1800 3½% War Loan at 108¾%	£1957	10	0
£500 3½% Conversion Loan at 111%	555	0	0
Balance at credit with agent	3	9	3
	£2515	19	3

	£	s	d		£	s	d
Divisible thus :—							
Mr John Johnston—one-third	£838	13	1				
Miss Joan Johnston—one-third . . .	838	13	1				
Miss Elizabeth Mary Johnston—one-third . .	838	13	1				
					£2515	19	3

The above sums will be met thus :—

	£	s	d		£	s	d
Mr John Johnston—							
£600 3½% War Loan at 108¾%					£652	10	0
£166 3½% Conversion Loan at 111%					184	5	2
Cash					1	17	11
					£838	13	1
Miss Joan Johnston—							
£600 3½% War Loan at 108¾% . . .	£652	10	0				
£167 3½% Conversion Loan at 111% . .	185	7	5				
Cash	0	15	8				
					838	13	1
Miss Elizabeth Mary Johnston—							
£600 3½% War Loan at 108¾% . . .	£652	10	0				
£167 3½% Conversion Loan at 111% . .	185	7	5				
Cash	0	15	8				
					838	13	1
					£2515	19	3

CHAPTER XVI

AUDITS

TRUST audits may vary in their size, but the general principles are common to all. An audit involves the scrutiny of the whole administration of the trust funds, under the powers and duties given to the trustees in the trust disposition.

The auditor is appointed by the trustees and their minutes should record his appointment. The factor should send him the account under audit along with the following documents :—

(1) Previous year's account.

Productions.

(2) Vouchers (as detailed below).
(3) Minute book (or Sederunt Book) containing copies of minutes of trustees, will, confirmation, etc.
(4) Signed minutes of trustees prepared during the period under audit.
(5) Letters and computations *re* income tax assessments and claims, with copies of returns.
(6) Leases of heritable property and rental with full particulars of rents and expenses.
(7) Feu-chartulary showing feuduties receivable.
(8) Evidence that annuitants and liferenters are still alive—such as certificates of life signed by an independent person, or letters from the beneficiaries may be accepted if the signatures are known.
(9) Factor's account-current, showing cash transactions in order of date.

In a first audit the auditor also requires the following documents :—

(1) Will of testator. A copy of this document or a full abstract of it should be retained by the auditor.
(2) Confirmation of executors.
(3) Valuations of heritable property and furniture as at date of death, and roup roll for furniture sold. If furniture is liferented, the liferenter should acknowledge in writing that he holds it in terms of the will and does not claim absolute ownership.
(4) Copy of estate duty inventory.

As regards cash transactions it is necessary to see a voucher for every item. Heritable properties sold and purchased are vouched by solicitors' states for settlement. Rents of properties, where there are local factors, are vouched by their accounts which should be rendered half-yearly, and expenses such as rates, taxes, and repairs are checked with receipted statements. The auditor should see whether all rents have been received in accordance with the leases and rental, and enquiry ought to be made regarding any arrears. Bad debts should be written off, leaving only genuine arrears in the accounts. Repairs and other

Vouchers.
(1) Heritable
Properties.

147

outlays may be partly recoverable from adjoining proprietors, and it should be seen whether they have been claimed. It should be observed whether all burdens, such as feuduties, rates, taxes and insurance premiums have been duly paid. (The insurance policies should be examined.) Local rates and income tax schedules A and B should usually be charged only on the actual rental.

(2) Investments.

Investments sold and purchased are vouched by stockbrokers' contract notes. If a bond is paid up, the discharged bond and disposition should be seen, and partial repayments should be endorsed on the bond. Income on investments is checked with dividend counterfoils, but, *e.g.* War Loan interest can only be verified by calculation as no counterfoils are issued. Interest on deposit receipts can be checked with certificates of interest issued by the bank, and interest on deposit accounts with the pass-books. The auditor must be satisfied that all due income has been received. *The Stock Exchange Official Year Book* gives particulars of dividends and bonuses of most public companies, and as regards private companies and partnerships the audited accounts must be examined. Profits and drawings from partnerships should be reconciled with their accounts. Where trusts have interests in other trusts, the audited accounts of these ought also to be seen.

(3) Charities.

In auditing the accounts of a charity the subscriptions received are vouched with counterfoil receipt books, and checked in total with the annual list of subscriptions. Copies of the latter should be printed and sent to all subscribers as a further check.

(4) Death Duties.

Death duty assessments and receipts are checked with the estate duty inventory, and legacy and succession duty accounts, and the allocation of duty should be verified. On any death affecting the trust funds the auditor calls for clearance certificates to be issued by the Estate Duty Office, so that it may be seen whether further duties have fallen due and remain unpaid.

(5) Income Tax.

Income tax assessments and claims are checked, and the auditor should see whether returns of untaxed income and all possible claims for recovery of tax have been made and properly settled.

(6) Management Expenses.

The solicitors' legal business accounts may be remitted by the trustees to the auditor, or alternatively to the Auditor of Court for taxation. (In Edinburgh this is the Auditor of the Court of Session, and elsewhere the Sheriff Court Auditor. In Glasgow, the Auditor of the Faculty of Procurators taxes business accounts.) In the latter circumstances, when auditing the trust account, no further examination is required beyond checking the total and allocation into the account. When taxing business accounts an auditor will have before him the Table of Fees for Conveyancing and General Business, and he should see that no charges are in excess of the scale. Commission on cash transactions is also fixed by reference to the same Table, and in doing so it is necessary to take into account any commission already received by the factor, *e.g.* as share of stockbrokers' commission or on allotment of debentures. A receipt should be seen for any fees charged by solicitors whether in a business account or as commission. It is important to see that no remuneration is paid to trustees, either directly or indirectly, unless specifically authorised by the trust disposition.

(7) Beneficiaries.

Payments to beneficiaries should all be formally acknowledged. Receipts for legacies and annuities are usually obtained on payment, but, in the case of a liferent, a formal letter acknowledging that the whole income has been received must be signed by the liferenter after the income balance is ascertained on closing the accounts. Any over-payments should be noted and referred to in the report.

Stamped receipts are of course required for all payments, unless specifically exempt such as wages, salaries, income tax and government duties. After all the vouchers have been checked, a list of missing vouchers is included in the notes on the audit, which are submitted to the factor for his attention. (8) General.

The investments of the trust are checked from the confirmation, which shows moveables in the United Kingdom; details of other property are compared with copies of the estate duty inventory and corrective inventories. These also show debts due by deceased and funeral expenses, which should be reconciled with the account. First Audits.

The trust account and account-current summations should be checked, and the balance remaining at the close of the period is compared with the factor's cash account in his ledger. If there is a separate bank account for the trust it should be noted that all cash has been paid in throughout the period, and no balances retained by the factor. The balance at the close should be certified by the bank. If there is no bank account, interest should be allowed to the trust on any balance in hands of the factor, which, however, should be a reasonable sum—any large balance being at once lodged on deposit receipt. Conversely, interest may be charged by the factor on any advances by him. It is not advisable for the trustees to borrow from a bank or from the factor except for temporary reasons, and the auditor should see whether they have, in fact, power to borrow on security of the trust funds. Bank and Cash Balances.

As to the administration of the trust, the auditor should see whether the trustees have carried out the trust purposes, and that they have not exceeded their powers. The minutes should be checked into the account, noting whether all decisions have been properly recorded and executed, and also observing whether anything has been omitted from the minutes. There may be questions as to legal rights of beneficiaries and the factor should produce documentary evidence when these have been waived. Trustees' Administration.

Advances to beneficiaries on account of residue should be minuted and must not exceed sums authorised in the will. No advances should be made to a minor beneficiary without his curator's consent.

Apportionments and allocations between capital and income must be checked. The account should show clearly the capital and income balances at the close of the account, and a complete list of all investments at that date must be given. The auditor compares this with the list of investments at the beginning of the period under audit, allowing for sales and purchases. A note should be made of any unauthorised investments, and these should be referred to in the auditor's report. Where the account does not show the current value of the investments in detail, mention should be made in the report of any outstanding depreciation in value of the holdings. Details in Accounts.

A list of notes on the audit can now be prepared for answer by the factor, in which list should appear all questions not satisfactorily dealt with in the accounts. It is convenient to state the questions on the left side of the page so that the respective answers may be placed opposite. Notes on Audit.

When answers are received, a list of supplementary notes arising from these may require to be sent to the factor. It is the auditor's duty to include in his report particulars of any points on which complete satisfaction is not obtained. As regards minor questions, it may, however, be sufficient for the factor to give a written agreement to make any necessary adjustments in the next account.

Examination of Securites.

The examination of securities is usually carried out at the factor's office. Certificates should be initialled by the auditor. Investments in Scottish companies should be registered in names of the trustees as such and not as individuals. English companies do not usually recognise trusts, and investments registered in individual names should be detailed in a formal acknowledgment of trust signed by the trustees. As regards inscribed stocks, verifications are required from the registrars at the time of each audit, as the stock certificates are worthless for audit purposes. Other stock certificates require to be surrendered on sale, but this does not apply to inscribed stocks. Bearer certificates should be certified by the banks holding them as being held for the trustees, with all future coupons attached. Dispositions of heritable property in favour of the trustees (or the testator) should be seen, although it is not part of an auditor's duty to examine in detail the titles of such property. The solicitor should certify that all the titles are in his possession and are in order. Where there are heritable bonds, the agents for the lenders hold the titles to the property over which the bonds are secured, and a certificate to this effect is required in auditing the accounts of both borrower and lender. In auditing the lender's accounts the receipts for feuduty and fire insurance premium receipts should be seen, as the right to the property might lapse if these payments were not kept up. It should be noted that bonds are not in excess of two-thirds of the value of the property. Formal acknowledgments by each borrower, confirming the amounts still outstanding and stating the current rate of interest, may be called for by the auditor. This is recommended as the most satisfactory method of guarding against the omission of partial repayments.

Where investments have been realised after the close of the accounts but before the audit is carried out, the auditor should see contract notes for the sales and evidence as to banking or re-investment of the proceeds.

Report.

A report on the audit should be drafted, containing an abstract of the accounts, and referring to all points as to which satisfaction has not been obtained or which in the auditor's opinion require the trustees' attention. This report should be submitted to the factor for comment before extension, and it may be desirable to modify the wording as suggested by him. The auditor then docquets the account " Referred to in my report of this date " (or similar wording) and signs his report, which may be in the following style :—

> REPORT by JOHN JOHNSTON, C.A., on the accounts of the Trustees of the late Miss AGNES WILSON who resided at 48 Meadow Walk, Edinburgh.
> From 31st January 1932
> To 31st January 1933.

Miss Agnes Wilson died at Edinburgh on 31st January 1932, leaving a trust disposition and settlement dated 18th December 1918 with codicil dated 11th February 1922, whereby she disponed her whole estate to Messrs William Wilson and George Wilson, and the survivor, as executors and trustees for the following purposes :—

(1) To pay all lawful debts, deathbed and funeral expenses, and the expenses of trust administration.
(2) To pay the following legacies free of duty six months after the date of death.
(Here detail these.)

(3) To pay the free annual income of the remainder of the estate to her sister, Miss Margaret Wilson.
(4) On the death of Miss Margaret Wilson, to transfer the residue of the estate to the Edinburgh Royal Infirmary.

Both the trustees nominated accepted office and they appointed Mr Thomas Brown, W.S., to be their solicitor and factor. The trust disposition and settlement was recorded in the Books of Council and Session on 10th February 1932, and an inventory of the estate was prepared for estate duty purposes showing estate of £5748, 6s. 3d.

The trustees completed their title to the whole heritable and moveable property belonging to deceased, and paid all government duties. The trustees have carried out the first two purposes of the trust, and have made payments of £100 in all to Miss Margaret Wilson on account of income, leaving a balance of £36, 3s. 2d. due to her as at 31st January 1933, as shown in the Abstract of Accounts appended. All income receivable has been duly accounted for.

The trustees remitted the account of their intromissions for year to 31st January 1933 to me for audit and report, and I beg to state that I have examined the account and found it to be correctly stated and sufficiently vouched, closing with a balance of £82, 16s. 3d. due to the factor. The factor has taken credit for the following sums in respect of his professional charges, which I consider to be fair and reasonable :—

	Capital.	Income.
Business Account . . .	£42 0 0	£3 7 6
Commission on Cash Transactions .	10 10 0	7 17 6
	£52 10 0	£11 5 0

I have examined the securities for the investments held as at the close of the account, as to which the following points have been noted for the information of the trustees :—

(1) No valuation has been exhibited to me in respect of the heritable property, 88 Meadow Walk, Edinburgh, over which £800 is held in Bond and Disposition in Security.
(2) There is an uncalled liability on the investment in 30 A shares Lloyds Bank of £5 each £1 paid.
(3) The following investments are in bearer form, and are held by the factor :—

300 shares common stock Shell Union Oil Corporation.
£50 4% Victory Bond.

(4) A certificate has been granted by the factor in respect of the titles to the heritable property held by him, stating that these are in order.

(5) No income has been received from the Shell Union Oil Corporation during the year.

Subject to these remarks the investments have been found to be in order. I have prepared the annexed Abstract of the Accounts of the trustees for year to 31st January 1933.

(Here follows a summary of the accounts.)

Reported by

(Signed)   JOHN JOHNSTON, C.A.

EDINBURGH, 10*th March* 1933.

Audits of Continuing Trust Accounts.

The audit of subsequent accounts is usually simpler than that of a first account. Similar principles are followed, however, and the productions required are as detailed above.

The funds must be checked from the list at close of the previous account. Notes on the last audit should be read, and items carried forward for attention must be cleared up. A list of notes may be required on the occasion of each audit, and, in practice, it is often necessary to ask the same questions year after year. Securities are examined in the same way as at the first audit, but certificates already seen and initialled do not require to be scrutinised so closely. The auditor should note whether changes in trustees have been intimated to the various companies.

It is important to notice whether the trustees have recently reconsidered the investments held, and if not, this should be mentioned in the report. Unauthorised investments must also be reported upon each year until they are realised.

When the audit has been completed, the auditor may prepare a detailed report as in the example above, and this is essential if the trust is complicated or the account is unsatisfactory. Alternatively, a docquet may be appended to the account certifying that it is in order, as in the following example :—

Docquet.

GLASGOW, 10*th February* 1933.—I have examined the foregoing account of the intromissions of X and Y as factors for the trustees of the late A B for the year to 1st January 1933, which I have found to be correctly stated and sufficiently vouched. I have examined the securities for the investments and found them in order and satisfied myself that all income arising has been duly accounted for. The factors have taken credit for the following sums in respect of their professional services, and these charges are, in my opinion, fair and reasonable :—Business account £52, 6s. 8d., commission on cash transactions £110, making £162, 6s. 8d. in all. The account closes with a balance of £26, 7s. 3d. due to the factors.

(Signed)   ALEXANDER JOHNSTON, C.A.

Audits of Final Accounts and Schemes of Division.

In auditing final trust accounts, in addition to the usual audit programme, the auditor should observe that all outstanding death duties, taxes, and expenses have been included in the account, and should see the clearance certificates regarding death duties and income tax.

The will or other deed constituting the trust should be re-examined to see whether all the trust purposes have been carried out. As regards those persons who share in the division of the estate, the auditor must be satisfied that none is omitted and that all advances have been correctly included. The auditor should see proof of death of beneficiaries who have died before the vesting of their legacies. The revaluation of the funds for division should be checked and the allocation of the investments examined. If requested, the share transfers may be checked by the auditor.

After the auditor has completed his examination of the scheme of division he appends a docquet stating that he has found it in order, as in the following style :—

EDINBURGH, 10th February 1933.—I have examined and audited the Docquet. foregoing Scheme of Division of the estate of the late John Jones as at 1st January 1933, and I have verified the prices and calculations included there. I have found the figures to be correct, and in accordance with the trust purposes.

(Signed)   JOHN JOHNSTON, C.A.

INDEX

PRINTED IN GREAT BRITAIN BY
OLIVER AND BOYD LTD.
EDINBURGH